TERENCE LESTER

FOREWORD BY **FATHER GREGORY BOYLE**

WHEN WE STAND

THE POWER OF SEEKING JUSTICE TOGETHER

An imprint of InterVarsity Press
Downers Grove, Illinois

InterVarsity Press
P.O. Box 1400, Downers Grove, IL 60515-1426
ivpress.com
email@ivpress.com

InterVarsity Press® is the book-publishing division of InterVarsity Christian Fellowship/USA®, a movement of students and faculty active on campus at hundreds of universities, colleges, and schools of nursing in the United States of America, and a member movement of the International Fellowship of Evangelical Students. For information about local and regional activities, visit intervarsity.org.

Scripture quotations, unless otherwise noted, are from the New Revised Standard Version Bible, copyright © 1989 National Council of the Churches of Christ in the United States of America. Used by permission. All rights reserved worldwide.

Published in association with Tawny Johnson of Illuminate Literary Agency, www.illuminateliterary.com.

While any stories in this book are true, some names and identifying information may have been changed to protect the privacy of individuals.

The publisher cannot verify the accuracy or functionality of website URLs used in this book beyond the date of publication.

Cover design and image composite: David Fassett
Interior design: Daniel van Loon
Image: half-tone dot pattern: © Aerial / iStock / Getty Images Plus

ISBN 978-0-8308-3178-4 (print)
ISBN 978-0-8308-3179-1 (digital)

Printed in the United States of America ∞

InterVarsity Press is committed to ecological stewardship and to the conservation of natural resources in all our operations. This book was printed using sustainably sourced paper.

Library of Congress Cataloging-in-Publication Data

A catalog record for this book is available from the Library of Congress.

P 25 24 23 22 21 20 19 18 17 16 15 14 13 12 11 10 9 8 7 6 5 4 3 2 1

Y 41 40 39 38 37 36 35 34 33 32 31 30 29 28 27 26 25 24 23 22 21

"This provocative piece by my friend Terence Lester is both a motivational journal of his personal call to action and events that he could not ignore, and a model journey into a collective call that we can share. Now is the time to act, and *When We Stand* is the pathway to action."
William K. Gravely, lead pastor of Refuge Community Church, Austell, Georgia

"He has experienced homelessness and now he's helping the rest of us draw near to those we might otherwise fear, scapegoat, and want to blame. If you care about justice and the transformation of your own biases at the intersection of personal dignity and structural change, Terence Lester is a leader to follow."
Jeremy Courtney, CEO of Preemptive Love and author of *Love Anyway*

"If reading the news, scrolling through social media, or watching current events unfold on television leaves you despairing and feeling helpless, *When We Stand* is the book for you. It's a must-read, offering a tangible and compelling way forward for everyone who wants to follow in the steps of our God of justice."
Karen González, immigrant advocate and author of *The God Who Sees*

"*When We Stand* is a poetic expression grounded in a faith-based perspective addressing a multitude of social injustices and worldly misfortunes. Terence's vision of interconnection and call for action is simply remarkable."
Alieizoria Redd, executive director of Covenant House Georgia

"Through vulnerability, conviction, and empathy, Terence Lester clearly lights a path to what togetherness can look like on this never-ending journey to justice. *When We Stand* invites us to see ourselves the way God does: as a unified body, with each person having a specific and valuable role to play in the larger story."
Danielle Coke, digital illustrator and activist

"Using faith as both his fuel and fire, Terence Lester solidifies his place and voice as a national leader in homeless advocacy and human rights in his new book *When We Stand*. He brings a clear message of faith and purpose—cutting through the clutter of news cycles and social media noise—and reminds us that humanity, and the love we have for it, is the only way to truly seek justice and obtain it together."
DeMark Liggins, national chief of staff, Southern Christian Leadership Conference

"Through powerful story that is rooted in Scripture, Lester challenges us to become proximate to the injustices of this world, because it's only when we've encountered these pains close and upfront that we will begin to understand, care, and seek to do something about it. Lester's life and ministry are a testament to this, and I can't think of a better person to serve as a guide to one of the most important conversations of our age."

Michelle Ami Reyes, co-executive director of Pax and vice president of the Asian American Christian Collaborative

"When We Stand is a unique call and challenge for Christians living in the internet age. The antidote to compassion fatigue, being overwhelmed, or loneliness, as Lester beautifully illustrates, is not more stuff on your to-do list but deeper practice of proximity, vulnerability, and consistency. This book is a vital word for all of us."

Chad Wright-Pittman, associate pastor for care and outreach at First Presbyterian Church of Anderson, South Carolina

"Terence's brilliant understanding of the gospel in action comes to life in this book. This book is my walking bible as I go into the world to heed the call of God to make the world the just world that God intended. This works calls me to see, act, feel, and do something about what I see in the world that is unjust, immoral, and deprives my brothers and sisters of the full life that they were created to live."

Ralph Basui Watkins, Peachtree Professor of Evangelism and Church Growth at Columbia Theological Seminary, Decatur, Georgia

"Terence has committed his life to helping others know they are seen, heard, and that each of us has purpose regardless of our circumstances. In *When We Stand,* Terence helps us discover how we can be a part of collective change. His words are real and honest truths that challenge us deeply. This book is an essential to our souls if we want to see change in our current day."

Eryn Eddy, author, founder of So Worth Loving

"Lester names an age-old solution to the barriers that keep us from playing a meaningful role in positive change and draws a map to help us get there. As someone who knows firsthand the lands we must traverse, Terence doesn't just point a finger toward our desired destination but serves as a guide for the journey."

Rob Kaple, lead pastor of Grace Midtown Church in Atlanta

"When I hear my friend Terence Lester speak, I feel as if I'm listening to one of the civil rights prophets of fifty years ago. He is passionate, humble, and has a deep care for the poor and marginalized. That same world-changing energy comes through in *When We Stand*. To a culture that often appears unwell, this book feels like a welcome medicine."

B. T. Harmon, creative strategist and podcaster

"*When We Stand* is a book the world needs right now. There's a lot of talk about how to fix the issues that plague us, but very little action to match. What I love about my brother Terence's amazing book is that he doesn't just talk the talk; chapter by chapter we follow him as he goes into the dark places of society operating as an agent of change, and then he utilizes his experiences to paint a blueprint for the reader."

Remi Adeleke, author and actor

"Terence Lester is a champion for the image of God found in every human— not just those worshiping next to us on Sunday. *When We Stand* is a beautiful challenge to honor God through our acts of restorative justice."

Brandy Wallner, writer and founder of A Good Conversation Dinner

"*When We Stand* is a mosaic of practical wisdom that does not endeavor for us to add to our already overflowing to-do list but empowers us with tools that create space to do justly. The hope is that we stop talking about doing justice and actually work alongside existing community advocates. As Terence says, 'When we stand together, we can make this world a significantly better place.'"

Gricel Medina, pastor and church planter, the Evangelical Covenant Church

"For those who take seriously the call to put faith into action and be salt and light in this world, Terence's words and wisdom here will give us much guidance. He has lived the truth he speaks, and his words are prophetic and powerful yet seasoned with grace and delivered with love. May the Holy Spirit move in you and through you as you read *When We Stand*."

Susie Gamez, speaker and writer

"Terence Lester taps into a macro problem in our increasingly virtual society—the weight of seeing how people are being mistreated all over the world. We are more aware of injustice. That awareness can be overwhelming. *When We Stand* comforts the hearts and guides the minds of those who want to move past awareness into action."

Darrell Hall, pastor and intergenerational communication expert

"*When We Stand* is for those who feel overwhelmed by all the suffering and injustice people are experiencing in our country and around the world. When Terrence Lester speaks, I'm listening because he draws from his lived experience, not just untested abstract propositions. This book is a gift from a credible witness."

Drew G. I. Hart, assistant professor of theology at Messiah University and author of *Who Will Be a Witness?*

"Doing the hard work of change requires locking arms with others. Terence is one of those courageous friends to me. This book is the guide for justice work, together."

Jeff Shinabarger, founder of Plywood People and author of *Love or Work*

"When Terence writes something down, I need to read it because Terence embodies his truth. His heart has always been for the one not commonly seen. In *When We Stand*, Terence helps us to reimagine justice through the eyes of a community. You'll be challenged to do the hard work with others!"

Dave Gibbons, advisor and activist

"*When We Stand* is an invitation into the dream that brings us closer to God, whose life-giving breath infuses dignity, agency, and communal flourishing. May we be brave enough to dream as Terence has and humble enough to follow his lead."

Gena Thomas, author of *Separated by the Border*

"Terence has done it again! The passion of leaders like Terence make it possible for works of art to exist that both challenge individualism while offering a solution for isolation—When We Stand is that work of art. Do yourself a favor and explore this vital portrait of how together we can create a masterpiece."

Tedashii, artist, author, and speaker

THIS BOOK IS DEDICATED TO ALL OF THE PEOPLE WHO GENUINELY WANT TO SEE A BETTER WORLD. It's for the misfit who hasn't found a space where they belong, the creative who is working to solve problems, and the innovator who has ideas about how things should be different—and is actively trying to achieve that goal.

THIS BOOK IS FOR THE REBEL who stirs up, as the late John Lewis said, "a good kind of trouble" because the change that they desire is needed to achieve justice. It's for the out-of-the-box thinker and the people of faith who truly believe in the power of building longer tables at which we will all break bread together—instead of building higher walls that keep us from the humanity of togetherness.

THIS BOOK IS ALSO FOR THE MEMBERS OF CHURCHES WHO AREN'T AFRAID TO GET THEIR HANDS DIRTY by taking the good news of God outside the four walls of the church, into the places that Chicago pastor Johnathan Brooks calls "forsaken."

THIS BOOK IS FOR THE ORGANIZATIONS THAT ARE IN THE TRENCHES doing the hard work that no one wants to do, for the individuals who are working hard in the local community to give people hope, and for the dreamers who dare to risk it all to ensure that justice and mercy prevail for every person. I hope that after reading the words on these pages, each of you finds a renewed sense of vision and hope to continue the journey and to be a part of the Great Commission. Your work—as an individual—matters. Most importantly, though, your work *together* makes the world a better place.

CONTENTS

The Spirit of the Lord is upon me,
because he has anointed me
to bring good news to the poor.
He has sent me to proclaim release to the captives
and recovery of sight to the blind,
to let the oppressed go free,
to proclaim the year of the Lord's favor.

LUKE 4:18-19

FOREWORD

Father Gregory Boyle

I met Terence Lester on a panel in Atlanta. He spoke of Love Beyond Walls; I shared details about Homeboy Industries: a gang intervention program I founded thirty-two years ago in Los Angeles. At one point, Lester told us how much fruit he'd gained from Henri Nouwen's writings. I then mentioned, on the panel, that Nouwen had been my professor at Harvard Divinity School. Suddenly, we connected. I shared Nouwen's sentiment that ministry is simply a willingness to "receive" people.

When We Stand helps us all to connect. The homies at Homeboy Industries say, "We are used to being watched. We aren't used to being seen." This book helps us imagine exactly the kind of thing that Love Beyond Walls practices. It articulates the principles of a movement where we "see" people and "receive" them. It asks us to see the folks who are on the margins: the abandoned and the despised, the demonized and the disposable. This dynamism, both seeing and receiving, restores us all to a state of dignity and to our

inherent nobility. *When We Stand* alters our hearts; things
then settle for us . . . first things recognizably first. We
choose to live in each other's hearts. We are connected—as
surely as Terence and I were on that panel a long time ago.

I write this during "World War C"—the era of the
Covid-19 crisis. During this time, we are all together . . . at
home. As a homie said to me, "Our physical doors are
locked, but our spiritual doors are wide open." A homegirl
texted me, terrified of the isolation: "I'm afraid I'm gonna
lose it." I told her, "No . . . you're going to gain it." By "it," I
meant a newfound resilience, an expansive sense that
we're all in this together, a spacious new way to be a community. We'll gain all that.

Terence Lester, his work and his writing, reminds me of
the Zen saying: "The finger pointing to the moon . . . is not
the moon." Terence points to it. He signposts this larger
love, beyond himself—and beyond our own self-absorption.
Terence invites us to embrace a love that is without measure
and without regret. It connects us. And therein lies our
joy—even in a time of uncertainty and pandemic.

In such times, we rely on a voice like Terence Lester's. It
beckons us to joy, in spite of everything. It knows what can
scale the walls that divide and keep us from each other. It
widens the circle and we're astounded at how thrilling it is
when we know, finally, that our separation has always been
an illusion. We are meant, after all, to embrace kinship and
connection. We are grateful to have been reminded. In precisely this way, Terence Lester is the shape of God's heart.

INTRODUCTION

BE BETTER–TOGETHER

Right now, you have every injustice in the world at your fingertips. At this very moment, billions of people all around the globe are accessing content that has been shared on social media platforms with ease from their smartphones or the latest technological device. In many ways, our technology has become an intricate part of our daily lives. What content have you viewed in the last few moments? Think about it. While some people in the world are using technology to keep in touch with relatives, family, and friends—sharing pictures and videos that help to close the distances between loved ones—another trend has simultaneously been emerging. We're all posting content that relates to injustices and disasters on social media, which means our awareness of the problems that exist in the world is ever increasing.

It's the start of a new decade—and we have already witnessed fires burn down parts of Australia and claim lives, two impeachment trials of the president of the United States and his ordering a missile attack inside Iran, news about children being taken away from their parents at the border, major storms displacing people in Puerto Rico, the spread of Covid-19, and the increased awareness of the racial divide in the United States. None of these headlines, though, seem to include the ways that people are responding to the issues of poverty or economic inequality, or the effects of war, slavery, or violence, with offerings of help. We seem to be inundated with bad news without being given much hope of anything ever changing. Just last week, I came across an article that had been posted on social media about a man who—though experiencing homelessness —had even been evicted from the woods.[1]

Right now, many of us are consuming information at such a rapid rate that we feel overwhelmed by the sheer extent and constant reminders of injustice. According to media agency Sproutworth, in 2019, "71% of people [had] increased their online video viewing," and "150 million people are using Facebook Stories."[2] As we as a society become increasingly connected due to technological advances, the speed with which we are able to access world news will continue to increase, thereby heightening our levels of awareness of injustice.

When I use the word *injustice*, I'm referring to any systemic issue that threatens, robs, or blocks a person from reaching their God-given potential or prohibits them from experiencing equal and equitable treatment or access. Having been exposed to so much content related to injustice, it can be all too easy to simply disengage, feel numb, or become confused about what we can do to make a difference. We begin to ask deflating questions like, "What can we do about it?" or "Is it even possible for me to change this?"

APATHY OR ACTION?

If you are like me, you can probably remember where you were when you found out from your cellphone about some type of injustice that was occurring in our world. I remember exactly where I was when I received the alert on my phone about the church shooting that took place in Charleston, South Carolina, during a Bible study group session at Emanuel African Methodist Episcopal Church. I was just leaving the gym, and there it was on the screen: "Dylann S. Roof and the Charleston Church Massacre."[3] Finding out about it there—alone—I remember the rage that I felt and the tears that accompanied my immense frustration. It was paralyzing.

I was trying to figure out why we're still wrestling with racial injustice in our country, and in our world, in the post–civil rights era. I was even more frustrated by this unwelcome reminder that we allow almost anyone to access weapons in places where violence and mass shootings can occur all too easily; I couldn't understand it. When I reached my car, I yelled out loud: "Nine people lost their lives because we have an issue with guns and racism in our country!"

You probably have similar stories of how updates from that little device called a cellphone have caught you off-guard in recent years—and left you feeling isolated when confronted with the world's problems. After a while, we can start to feel apathy creeping in from all the social media trauma. It can cause us to internalize our grief and never speak out against these issues, or be swept up by our frustrations, venting to our friends and family while never really engaging with possible solutions.

Conversely, we could stand up and fight against these injustices. It often takes only a spark of an idea or a shift in our perspective to reach a point at which we finally assert that "enough is enough." That's what happened for me in 2013 as I walked through the downtown Atlanta area with several Christian friends of mine, heading toward a Christian event. I vividly remember the disappointment I felt listening to them make demeaning comments about the homeless population we passed on the street that night. I was saddened by my brothers in the faith; they hadn't realized their good news reaches beyond the four walls of the church. They were identical to the priest and the Levite whom Jesus spoke about in the parable of the Good Samaritan who passed by the injured man with no regard for the fact that he was half dead on the side of the road (Luke 10:25-37). Here my friends were, on their way to a conference to learn more about Jesus, not realizing that if Jesus were living, he'd be on the streets with the very people whom they were dehumanizing.

That moment would eventually lead to what is now Love Beyond Walls, a nonprofit organization that I lead in Atlanta. We focus on sharing stories of people who are struggling with homelessness in ways that deconstruct the false narratives that surround them and building relationships with people who have been overlooked. The organization would not have come to be had I not allowed that moment downtown and many other moments similar to that one to galvanize me toward taking action, one step at a time.

My point is not that you need to go out and start an organization. My point is, rather, that the world needs us to be moved by injustice, both emotionally and physically. Often injustice actually prompts feelings of apathy or a sudden desire to stick our heads in the sand and to hide from it all. The most powerful movements are those that require us to partner in community with others to stand and seek justice together. We must admit that encountering injustice is both traumatic and challenging for one person to carry and handle alone.

WE NEED EACH OTHER

By ourselves, the injustice and abuse of sex trafficking seem like a mountain that can never be conquered. By ourselves, when facing the issue of homelessness we feel as though we're peering into a bottomless pit of despair. For us to transition out of a state of despair and into a state in which we're ready to take action, we must start to build a community with others who also want to see the world changed for the better.

In 1983, during a commencement speech at Milton Academy in Massachusetts, Marian Wright Edelman, the head of the Children's Defense Fund, reminded students that they were all needed, together, because they were graduating at a time when the nation was experiencing moral and economic bankruptcy under an administration that used policy to hurt the poor. She urged students with these words: "Pick a piece of the problem that you can help [to] solve while trying to see how your piece fits into the broader social change puzzle."[4] I would add that as we move forward in trying to build that community, we must also exercise a little introspection and ask ourselves some hard questions. I'll address those hard questions within the pages of this book. However, I do believe that one of the greatest enemies in the context of seeking to move forward and to make a difference is not a shortage of resources but rather a lack of connection and community. Most of the pressing issues that exist in our world require the adoption of a multi-pronged, comprehensive, cohesive, and community-centered approach if they are to be solved. They require the gifts, skills, and talents of many different people. They necessitate a diverse range of perspectives and the inclusion of voices that often go unheard. They require the power of *we*.

If God sees us—humankind—as a body and as a family, then why wouldn't we embrace that same principle when spending time with one another or finding ways in which to address social issues? I know that it's not the normal language that is used every day to communicate the value of togetherness, but I'd like to draw your attention to the language that Paul the apostle uses in the Bible to help people understand this type of connection. He wrote in 1 Corinthians 12:12-14:

> For just as the body is one and has many members, and all the members of the body, though many, are one body, so it is with Christ. For in the one Spirit we were all baptized into one body—Jews or Greeks, slaves or free—and we were all made to drink of one Spirit.
>
> Indeed, the body does not consist of one member but of many.

Paul was writing to encourage believers to see themselves as part of a larger whole, with each member functioning in a specific and very important role. Martin Luther King Jr. used similar language when he spoke about seeing all of humanity as a *world house*.[5] Think about how different the world would be if people, churches, and groups really saw themselves as being part of God's community and global village, functioning and carrying the burden together and standing together. Paul was right when he implored us to see that we are God's representatives on earth in the form of a community. The key is to accept that all of the constituent parts of a body are required to work together for the body as a whole to function properly.

Think about your own body. The simplest action—such as taking a step or even reading this sentence—relies upon many body parts working together so that the action may be carried out. In the same way, even seemingly simple problems often require a number of people who have different skills to work together in order to solve them.

THE CALL TO WALK TOGETHER

Imagine people from different walks of life, denominations, and backgrounds all working together with a "we" mentality instead of a "me" mentality as they confront the injustices in their communities. What a sight it would be for others to witness how the whole body of Christ can work together to serve alongside each other, taking a stand against injustice and practicing presence in the midst of tension. Practicing presence means being actively engaged with the community and showing up for members in the community in tangible ways that supersede giveaways or feedings. It means that when you serve people the connection doesn't stop at some event that helped a few poor people. Presence is about deep connection and relationships. Presence could show up in the form of conversation, standing in solidarity with a community after the loss of a member or after a brutality case, spending time with a neighbor to remind them they aren't alone, visiting someone who is battling an illness, or just checking in with community members to let them know you are there. Presence is more about being than doing. Oftentimes, we underestimate the power of the ministry of presence, which is largely how Jesus lived his life.

What if we were to step over denominational guardrails to undertake significant restorative work in the name of

Jesus? As Father Greg Boyle wrote in his book *Barking to the Choir: The Power of Radical Kinship*:

> Beyond cure and healing, Jesus was always hopeful about widening the circle of compassion and dismantling the barriers that exclude. He stood with the sinner, the leper, and the ritually impure to usher in some new remarkable inclusion, the very kinship of God. Living the gospel, then, is less about "thinking outside the box" than about choosing to live in this ever-widening circle of inclusion.[6]

What if we were to focus not upon denominational differences or a "them versus us" mindset but rather upon Jesus as the bridge that unites us? Not only would we make serious strides as a community of believers, but we could forge greater connections with each other and effect good in the world. We would move past the use of Jesus as a weapon and instead start actually letting his lifestyle guide us in how to use proximity and presence to turn this world upside down for God in a spirit of radical togetherness.

In *this* book, you will find out more about how we can *all* have a profound impact on the world and each other. You will also discover that for us to make this impact, we must create the space in our lives that we need in order to follow God's call into community and service to each other.

Something tells me, though, that the merits of a community coming together with their God-given gifts in order to bring about significant social change is not something that you need to be convinced of. If you've picked up this book, you probably already understand the importance of such work. But, for one reason or another, you have not been able to make this a reality in your own life as of yet. Perhaps, as I've already described, you feel overwhelmed by the mountains of injustice. Or maybe your schedule has never allowed you the space that you need to really get involved. You could even be a pastor who's struggling to motivate your church to love outside of its walls. This book is for anyone who is genuinely seeking to connect with other people in order to do what is needed to honor God and to change the world for the better through acts of service.

Along the way, I hope to challenge you—but my aim is not to add to your to-do list. If that's the message that you take away from this—that you have yet *another* thing to do—then I have failed in my endeavor. On the contrary, this is a book that will actually help you to remove a few items from your to-do list and process whatever you may need to work on internally in order for you to be ready to join others in making the world a better place.

Along the way, I'll point out what I believe to be hindrances to a life lived in community with one another, and a few challenges that keep people from seeking justice together in a healthy way. We'll discuss the concepts of busyness, unhealthy beliefs and patterns, the dangers of isolation, racism, and the false narrative of having nothing to offer. I want to help you carve out time for meaningful priorities and provide you with advice and practical steps for how you could become more involved in your local community and with other people who feel the same way that you do.

One of the greatest ways that people who don't know God themselves can nonetheless experience God's love is by seeing others operate in health and proximity, working together to be the hands and feet of God in this world. I hope that this book motivates you to make a long-term commitment to live according to God's call for us to come alongside others—to fight injustice and to invite others to join you in doing so. Be in no doubt that your work and your contributions matter and are even more profound when they're paired with the contributions of others in a spirit of community.

When we stand together, we can make this world a significantly better place.

CHAPTER ONE

GET OUT OF YOUR BUBBLE

An email from the principal of a private school in Atlanta arrived in my inbox. In the email, he stated that he wanted his students to learn to see outside of their immediate "bubble." As soon as I read those words, I knew what he was referring to. Being familiar with the school and the area in which it was located, I knew that the principal wanted me to speak to the school's affluent students about the importance of learning more about the world beyond their school environment.

The principal's email went into further detail and described what he meant by the word *bubble*. He wrote: "The students here at the school have tons of privileges like a well-appointed library, top-of-the-line technical resources, and educators with postgraduate degrees, and they have access to everything they could ever imagine and have no clue what is going on right outside the school. It's a bubble." From the tone and content of his email, I could discern not only the principal's feelings of frustration and his keen sense of urgency, but also his compassion and patience in wanting to

help his students understand the impact that they could
have on a local level if they were to embrace a sense of
awareness of, and proximity to, their local communities.

I accepted the engagement—not because I wanted to deliver a "guilt talk" to people with privileges, but because I
hoped to introduce the possibilities of what could happen if
these students and educators were to choose to step out of
isolation and join the community, which ultimately makes
the world around them a better place. It was the principal's
email that made me understand these words from the book
Tattoos on the Heart to a greater extent:

> Only kinship. Inching ourselves closer to creating a
> community of kinship such that God might recognize
> it. Soon we imagine, with God, this circle of com-
> passion. Then we imagine no one standing outside of
> that circle, moving ourselves closer to the margins so
> that the margins themselves will be erased. We stand
> there with those whose dignity has been denied.[1]

When the day arrived on which I was to deliver my talk
at the school, I remember vividly what I saw as I drove into
the community. Immediately I understood, in much more
depth, what the principal actually meant in his email.
While driving, I saw people experiencing homelessness.
They were pushing shopping carts down the street that
contained cans that they were hoping to trade for dollars.
I drove past boarded-up homes as well as gas stations at
which men were simply waiting around in the hopes of
finding work at a construction company. I also spotted

several apartment complexes that I knew were inhabited by those who were on extremely low incomes. I didn't notice a single grocery store on my journey. This meant that the local community was essentially a food desert. Was this the "The Other America" Martin Luther King Jr. spoke about in his speech given at Stanford University?[2]

I felt my heart breaking as I passed many people who were in desperate need—while I was embarking on a journey to a community that, in contrast, had everything that they could possibly need, as the principal had described in his email. *The opportunities for change are endless if this community would only push past isolation and get involved in building relationships with the community that surrounds them,* I thought. Finally, as I turned the next corner and started to get closer to the school itself, the contrast between the two communities became palpable. I could see that there were new homes in the area that were in the $370,000 to $395,000—if not above $400,000—price range. Construction was underway on more houses, and there were expensive cars in the driveways beside well-manicured lawns. It was as though I had entered a different world. What I later learned is that many families had actually relocated to the community and built homes specifically so that their children could attend this particular private school. The two communities were as different as they could possibly be. As the principal had warned, it felt like I was entering a bubble while gentrification was happening all around this neighborhood.[3]

Although the school and its immediate community were in proximity, geographically speaking, to the broader local community, they were mentally and spiritually miles apart from one another. Those who attended the school were essentially living in isolation—detachment—from people who were physically near them but were not "like them" in either financial or social terms. Many of the parents and students in this school had no idea that a number of the current residents in the community would be displaced years down the line because of the gentrification occurring due to wealthier families.

As a result of having the opportunity to speak with students at the school, I found myself compelled to think more broadly about the issue of isolation in our society that is, sadly, becoming more widespread.

COMING OUT OF ISOLATION

Isolation can feel safe. Perhaps it's what you've always known. It can feel, in many cases, comfortable and controllable. We go to work, talk to our group of friends, and live within our own family units. We have created our own bubbles that keep us from living lives that include building relationships with people from varying socioeconomic, cultural, or ethnic backgrounds. For many, including the students who attended the private school I spoke at, the idea of becoming involved with their neighbors felt uncomfortable. What did they have in common with the people staying at the local homeless shelter, after all? The idea that they would have anything in common with such people was completely foreign to them.

The kind of isolation in which the members of this school found themselves was not dissimilar to that which many of us who live in personal "bubbles" often experience. In a similar way, churches separate themselves from others because of denominational affiliations, territorialism, and competition, all in the name of the One who came to unite us: Jesus. Some church leaders find themselves in a "spiritual bubble" while at the same time professing a gospel that is supposed to bring us together. I remember personally speaking to one church leader who openly told me that they had no desire to work with a church that was less than a mile away because it would mean engaging with people who were "different" from those at his church.

As the church leader spoke, I couldn't help but wonder what God must think, given that so many churches operate like this leader. In addition to Paul's words about believers being one body (1 Corinthians 12:12-14), Scripture also calls believers to be priests, proclaiming the goodness of God to the nations:

> But you are a chosen race, a royal priesthood, a holy nation, God's own people, in order that you may proclaim the mighty acts of him who called you out of darkness into his marvelous light.
>
> Once you were not a people,
> but now you are God's people;
> once you had not received mercy,
> but now you have received mercy. (1 Peter 2:9-10)

How can believers come close to offering this hope of God's mercy to a world that is longing for it when we can barely seem to offer it to one another? It seems that, at every turn, believers are snapping at each other's heels on social media while forsaking a message of grace and welcome. Though we are asked not to judge one another, name-calling and finger-pointing are rampant; both apparently occur because of efforts to follow God's will. I wonder how often we encounter someone who has isolated themselves from the church because they found its people to be no different from those they already knew in the other parts of their life's world.

Those who isolate themselves do not seek to do so because of the extent of their privilege or status. Isolation has, in fact, offered a way in which they may protect themselves from what they perceive to be possible sources of risk, hurt, or danger in their lives. Some see isolation as a means of protecting their perceived worth and value in the eyes of others.

People also isolate themselves in order to deal with depression and other things that they struggle with. Sometimes, people crave solitude and become more guarded—putting up emotional walls—in order to try to avoid being hurt again after experiencing certain traumas. On a personal level, isolation is familiar to the human heart. It leaves us without connections, though, causing us to question many things, including ourselves. Too much isolation can lead to loneliness. Although they are two separate things, it is true that isolation can lead to feeling like you have no one there with you. Unsurprisingly, since humans were not meant for prolonged states of isolation, this can lead to major health concerns. According to health insurer Cigna, more than three in five Americans are lonely, with more and more people reporting that they feel that they are left out, poorly understood, and lacking in companionship.[4]

The rates of depression and suicide have skyrocketed across the nation. Although it's certain that chemical imbalances are partly responsible for such mental illnesses, experts insist that our widespread sense of disconnection is also a key factor. Though we live in a time when technology has produced a multitude of ways in which we might connect with one another, we seem to be missing an essential factor in connectivity—at substantial risk to our health. In 2018, an article in *Psychology Today* called the current scenario an "epidemic." Sharing Professor Julianne Holt-Lunstad's work on loneliness, the article stated, "Loneliness poses a serious physical risk—it can be, quite literally, deadly. As a predictor of premature death, insufficient social connection is a bigger risk factor than obesity and the equivalent of smoking up to 15 cigarettes a day."[5]

You may have felt the ache of loneliness that isolation brings. You may even feel it now. But you might also—simultaneously—feel hesitant about taking the initial steps toward joining a community. But what if we could all see the people "on the outside" who appear to be different from us as not really being all that different at all? What if we really believed that people around us are just like us because they, too, are part of the human family? It would change the ways in which we see ourselves, our communities, and our connections to those Jesus described as "our neighbors."

DISCOVER POWER IN PROXIMITY

Our hearts have been designed for the kind of kinship and connection that can only come from being in a community with other people. God knew from the very beginning that this type of existence would be the best one: an existence that helps to sustain, empower, and encourage others to live their best lives while simultaneously giving meaning to and enriching our lives. This is the miraculous gift of community. Without it, we're missing out on one of the biggest, most significant graces of being human.

In his now-famous "Letter from a Birmingham Jail," written in April of 1963, Reverend Dr. Martin Luther King Jr. spoke of our basic need to care for each other and to ensure one another's well-being. He asserted that the ability to safeguard each of our human rights is contingent on the human rights of another individual being upheld, regardless of their place in society, or regardless of what side of town they live on. In defense of his efforts to seek civil rights as an "outsider" in Birmingham, King said: "Injustice anywhere is a threat to justice everywhere. We are caught in an inescapable network of mutuality, tied in a single garment of destiny. Whatever affects one directly, affects all indirectly."[6]

King understood that, as individuals, we cannot even live a waking day without engaging in what he described as the "global village" or the "world house." He spoke of how connected we truly are—of how connected we ought to be—in his 1967 "Christmas Sermon on Peace" at Ebenezer Baptist Church:

Did you ever stop to think that you can't leave for your job in the morning without being dependent upon most of the world? You get up in the morning and go to the bathroom and reach over for the sponge, and that's handed to you by a Pacific Islander. You reach for a bar of soap, and that's given to you at the hands of a Frenchman. And then you go into the kitchen to drink your coffee for the morning and that is poured into your cup by a South American. And maybe you want tea: that's poured into your cup by a Chinese. Or maybe you desire to have cocoa for breakfast, and that's poured into your cup by a West African. And then you reach over for your toast, and that's given to you at the hands of an English-speaking farmer, not to mention the baker. And before you finish eating breakfast in the morning, you've depended on more than half the world. This is the way our universe is structured. It is its interrelated quality. We aren't going to have peace on Earth until we recognize this basic fact of the interrelated structure of all reality.[7]

Today, the same remains true. Pause for a moment in your reading and examine the labels on your clothing. Find out where your favorite shirt or dress was made. And while you're up, find out where the candle you burn to help you relax was produced. What about the decorative pillow on your couch? Your dining room table? Look much closer than the label and ask yourself who made the textiles. Where's the wax from? Where does this particular type of thread come from?

Recognizing that our lives are interconnected is the first necessary step in seeking to understand just how much we need each other, and our call to stand together. Community is necessary for us personally, but it is also a prerequisite for our considerations about how we might respond to— and try to solve—the issues and the injustices that we witness in the world. We need to understand this before we can take a stand and make any significant strides toward serving one another well. This is the main message that I wanted to convey to the private school students I spoke with—but it is also a message that we must *all* realize and come to recognize. I believe that this was the apostle Paul's main message when he wrote to the church in Corinth: "If one member suffers, all suffer together with it; if one member is honored, all rejoice together with it" (see 1 Corinthians 12:12-27).

When we start to see the world through a lens of *we,* we will fully grasp what Father Boyle means when he says: "There is no 'them' and 'us.' There is only us."[8] By understanding our need for one another and decreasing our levels of isolation, we can actually begin to enter into a spirit of community wholeheartedly, becoming proximate and present to our brothers and sisters who are in need: our neighbors.

One thing that I've discovered during my time working with communities is just how important the idea of— and the reality of embracing—proximity is.[9] Embracing proximity is not only the means by which we get closer to real-life issues but also how we enter into and develop deep relationships that could be beneficial to our own lives as we seek to achieve justice in the world. Accepting the need to live in proximity to others is how you become seen as an individual—as well as being, in turn, the way in which you have a chance to see and affirm the dignity of others. Being in proximity to people is how we connect with others to seek justice and change the world. Jesus connected with people whom he was proximate to, so why would it be any different for us? Scripture highlights Jesus' nearness to humanity in his ability to empathize and sympathize with our earthly sufferings: "For we do not have a high priest who is unable to sympathize with our weaknesses, but we have one who in every respect has been tested as we are, yet without sin. Let us therefore approach the throne of grace with boldness, so that we may receive mercy and find grace to help in time of need" (Hebrews 4:15-16).

Our lack of proximity to one another not only causes us to "otherize" people but it creates more division. No real solutions are developed when we are distanced from each other. In an article titled "Six Habits of Highly Empathetic People," researcher and author Roman Krznaric says: "Curiosity expands our empathy when we talk to people outside our usual social circle, encountering lives and worldviews very different from our own."[10] In fact, it is my belief that we have an empathy deficit and are in desperate need of this vital virtue to address the heaviness that we see in our communities and world.

Jesus made a lifestyle of connecting with those who were not like him. He ate with the misfits, the tax collectors, and the sinners. In his book *Accidental Pharisees: Avoiding Pride, Exclusivity, and the Other Dangers of Overzealous Faith,* author Larry Osborne says, "[Jesus'] goal was to expand the kingdom, to bring salvation to people who previously were excluded. He came to seek and find the lost, including a large group of folks no one else wanted to invite to the party. Everything about Jesus' ministry was designed to make salvation and the knowledge of God *more* accessible."[11]

When was the last occasion on which you made time to truly connect with someone over a meal whose worldview or status was vastly different from yours? When did you make an effort to serve someone without an agenda? When was the last time that you engaged in a meaningful conversation without trying to politicize the Messiah who came to give all for all?

GETTING CLOSE

As I reflect on my own life, I remember how embracing the values of proximity, vulnerability, and consistency not only served to tear down the walls that were isolating me but also provided a pathway for me to promote these principles among those around me. I was in high school, and struggling hard to find my identity. My father wasn't physically around much in my younger years, and though my mom worked hard to provide for us, I often felt that I was the cause of all of her frustrations. When I was seventeen years old, I remember leaving home because of tension and many times not feeling comfortable or accepted. My mom did all she could to raise a young Black man; my anger would not allow me to receive instructions from men that tried to talk to me who were not my own father. I was broken and couldn't understand why my family was too. Living anywhere other than my own home felt like a better solution, so I took to sleeping in the park. If I couldn't sleep in the park, I'd ask to stay on a friend's couch or floor. Before I knew it, I was a teenager experiencing homelessness from time to time.

On one particular night, I decided to use the little money that I had to call my friend Erik on a gas station payphone. When he picked up, I asked him if it would be possible to spend a night on his couch and to maybe have something to eat. Erik seemed hesitant at first but asked his father's permission anyway. When Erik got back on the line, I remember him saying, "Yeah, come on over—my family loves you."

Maybe I remember his words so clearly because they wound up being so profoundly true. Erik's father, Mr. Moore, would become one of my mentors and someone whose life embodied what it means to love sacrificially. That night, we formed a connection that would go on to last for years.

When I arrived at their family home that evening after a long drive, Mr. Moore came out to my car, carrying food for me. I remember him looking at me—and asking me to look at him. I also remember feeling, for the first time, that I could look at a man and that no harm would come to me—and that it was safe to just listen. I am forever grateful that I did so, because the moment that followed would change my life forever.

He looked at me earnestly and called me a leader.

A leader?

The word didn't seem to fit at all.

How could he say that when I was getting ready to go sleep in a park that night because I rebelled and ran away? Or when my teachers were kicking me out of their classrooms every day because I was falling asleep in lessons? I had issue after issue, all stemming from the circumstances in which I'd grown up, yet here was this man calling me a leader.

But when Mr. Moore said it, he meant it. He said that he saw something in me that no one else had. He'd seen the makings of a leader within me and had decided to speak to this capability. Even as I write this, I am deeply grateful. He passed away the very year that I started our organization

Love Beyond Walls. I wish that he could have seen the leader that I have become. He took the time to notice me— and to really *see* me—and that meant that the way in which I thought of myself slowly began to shift. Mr. Moore went on to become the person in my life I turned most frequently to when grappling with the big questions: "Should I put myself through college and work this job?" "Should I try and get involved with this ministry?" "Should I marry her?" He was even the person who encouraged me to start pursuing ministry and to try to start an organization. All of this transpired because he saw a young man who needed help and took what many would have considered to be too big of a risk. He saw the obstacles that I was experiencing and decided to become proximate. Mr. Moore showed me, in essence, a clear picture of the gospel, giving of himself in order for me to experience both love and restoration. His willingness to come close was more powerful than any sermon or lecture I could ever have received, and it provided the support that I needed to be able to navigate many of my greatest challenges. I wasn't an "other"; I was a part of his community.

It was proximity that also helped me understand my need for community. In recent years, it has helped me understand how important it is to address issues of injustice alongside other people. I believe that you can't fully understand a person and their struggles or affirm their humanity until you are proximate. People make judgments about people they have never met all the time and it is toxic. That's why Jesus modeled proximity when he chose to be among humanity. Jesus' proximity is actually what gave us life and affirmed our dignity, providing healing and connection to God.

VULNERABILITY

Though I was fortunate enough to have Mr. Moore come into my life while I was in high school, I ask myself why none of my teachers decided to find out what was really going on with me and in my life. All I can think of is that their actions were prohibited by their fear of sacrifice. My teachers were not bad people. Probing and entering into a student's or anyone's life, though, requires us to open ourselves up to potential hardship. Hardship produces hurts and those hurts can keep us from making ourselves vulnerable or make us not want to enter in to a relationship with someone that we want to walk with or help. It takes vulnerability of both sides to enter in to a space relationship or connection. So instead of entering into my life in a more personal capacity, my teachers sent me out of class—a lot. I got labeled for something that they did not understand and failed to ask about. However, God brought Mr. Moore into my life by way of helping to correct my path instead.

Our willingness to be open and to embrace vulnerability is key to being able to experience true connection at any level. Mr. Moore rendered himself vulnerable, and it was his vulnerability that helped me to overcome my isolation. This was the message that I hoped to impart to students through my talk at the private school. Years later, I am modeling that same type of vulnerability with others through our work with Love Beyond Walls. The aim of our organization is to love people who the rest of the world passes by and overlooks. People who are struggling with poverty have lives and stories that are just as valuable as ours. Fear should not stop any one of us from loving each one of them.

Beautiful things can happen when we emerge from our bubbles of isolation and step into the messiness of life. Though most people get into social justice work to "do something" for the betterment of their communities, what they realize over time is that very real work is being done inside of them as well. When Jesus said he came so that we may have life and have it to the full, it is this type of life that he meant (see John 10:10).

The part of us that hopes to remain at a distance from those in need due to our fear of the unknown is robbing us of the riches that are to be found within such relationships. We might feel good about our yearly visit to the local homeless shelter to serve dinner or about our year-end donation to an organization that works with youth in foster care. But that type of service is really more about how it makes the servant feel, rather than making a true difference to the recipient. Giving in such a spirit is nothing compared to what could happen to our hearts—and what we could potentially help to revive or to create—as a result of forging and strengthening social connections.

Our lives feel more meaningful and purposeful once we start to truly care about the people whom we once saw as being "separate" from us. This is largely because once we enter into a relationship, it's impossible to see someone as being altogether different from us. As a simple action step today, write down the names of your closest friends, family, and coworkers. Then think about how similar or dissimilar they are to you in terms of socioeconomic, cultural, and ethnic backgrounds. Think about ways that you can become closer to them and also ways you can step outside of your bubble to take steps toward knowing people more intimately or being proximate with those you have yet to meet. Ponder what discoveries you might make by doing this exercise.

If we are truly aiming to make the world better, we must be daring and bold enough to leave our isolated bubbles to both receive people and be received by those whom we have yet to fully meet. You can be close in space to a person and even causally talk to a person and not fully know them. If we are to fully allow proximity to shape our relationships, we must be willing to meet people on a deeper level. That means we must engage their world and allow them to engage our world as well. Taking a stand together means that we must actually be close to each other in ways that cause us to embrace vulnerability and authentic conversation, and move away from the isolation that keeps us separated from one another. A true mark of a follower of Jesus is not just having all the right things to say or doing things perfectly, but, like Christ, making our presence known with love, grace, truth, and proximity when everything seems to be going wrong in the world around us.

CHAPTER TWO

MAKE MORE TIME

When we are bombarded with activities that take up space in our lives, it leaves us no availability to join God's work in the world, connect with others well, or act justly against injustice. Have you ever felt that you were too busy to take care of yourself properly, let alone take advantage of opportunities to participate in the community in an authentic way? Or become involved in justice issues for that matter? I remember the exact day when I realized that I had too many things on my plate and that I needed to become more aware of how I allowed unnecessary things to take me away from doing activities that were important to me. I was in my early twenties and teaching in a local middle school in Atlanta. My routine that particular morning wasn't different from any other day. I arrived early to the school to prepare both my classroom and my lesson for the students, undertook some reading, and prepared session notes for an afterschool program called Trailblazers that I started for at-risk students.

However, that morning, something just didn't feel right. I felt as though I might be about to pass out. Because I was a young man, I didn't think that this feeling could possibly be related to my state of health. To be on the safe side though, I rang the front office and asked if the school nurse would come and check me over. She walked into my classroom and proceeded to ask me the normal questions that nurses ask in such circumstances:

"Mr. Lester, are you on any medication, or have you been stressed lately?" The room shrunk as I felt the weight of her words corner me.

"No. I don't think so." I responded with the type of caution that made my voice crack.

The nurse dug a little deeper. "Well, what do you have going on in your life? From what I notice, it seems like you always have a lot going on."

I could tell that her words came from a place of concern as she checked my vital signs.

I supposed that I did have a few things going on, and so I started to list them: "Well, my wife and I have a newborn baby and we were recently married. I am also in school for a graduate degree, full-time, I'm a youth pastor at a local church, I travel and speak, and I lead this afterschool program here with a couple of hundred students."

I stopped listing things because I could tell that she was wondering how in the world I was managing all that I had going on and still found time to breathe or genuinely connect with others. Her eyes were full of concern when

she asked me her next question: "Why are you trying to do
so much? Being extremely busy all the time doesn't necessarily mean that you are moving forward. Especially when
you are not caring for yourself. How can you truly care for
other people when you are too busy?" Caroline Beaton, a
columnist for *Forbes*, calls this "being sidetracked by
sudden time suckers that seem important but later leave
us empty-handed."[1]

I honestly didn't have a clear answer as to why I was
overloading my plate in the way that I was. The only thing
I could think of as a reason was that it seemed to me like
that was what everyone else was doing.

Busyness was what I saw glorified in culture every day
and in almost every area of life. When I watched television,
attended church, or even engaged in conversations, there
it was: people sharing messages, either indirectly or directly, about how—in order to be great or successful—you
must work nonstop, work your hardest every single day,
and literally never "let up." I had also seen my mom, as a
single parent, work very hard to provide for my sister and
myself. Somehow, the message that we ought to fill every
inch of our lives was embedded in my psyche. It was obvious that I believed that progress and worth were somehow
tied to keeping a full calendar and running oneself into the
ground in the process of doing so.

I think that the nurse said these things to me in that
moment because she truly cared about my longevity and
health. She was brave enough to say, "That is entirely too

much, even for a young man. You are placing yourself under too much pressure and your body is responding."

It's sad to say that the first time I ever had this type of conversation with anyone was with a nurse I barely knew while she was examining me in my own classroom. As she said those words, my body seemed to scream in agreement: *"I am tired."*

THE EFFECT OF BUSYNESS

Whether we will admit it or not, many people today find themselves in the same trap with the same messages playing in the background of their minds. Somehow, we have embraced the message that the way in which we ought to achieve validation and worth, to forge friendships, to make significant progress is by exhausting ourselves until we have nothing else to give—neither to ourselves nor to those around us. We cannot stand together or seek justice together if we have no time to do so.

I learned quickly that this is not the way in which God intended for us to live. It is definitely not a healthy lifestyle for anyone, let alone someone seeking to bring good into the world and to solve injustices. Being too busy keeps us from resting and prevents us from truly connecting with people around us.

In many cases, we are too busy to even know what is going on in the world or to even have time to formulate clear thoughts about what we think is going on about some issue that means a lot to us. Maybe we hear about it on a surface level on social media, or in passing from people whom we happen to be around, but when we are spread so thinly, we have no time to fully connect with or work together with others to undertake activities that would protect, promote, and achieve justice. At times I have engaged in conversations with people about injustices and found that they had formed opinions about things that they had not even researched or learned about in more depth. Many people have become too busy to even express the compassion they genuinely feel for others through action and verbal empathy. Rest, intentionality, and community are sacrificed on the altar of the American dream.

Several passages in the Bible literally speak of rest as a good and valuable asset to the human family. I think often of this passage from Matthew when I feel myself beginning to push and strive a little too hard: "Take my yoke upon you, and learn from me; for I am gentle and humble in heart, and you will find rest for your souls" (11:29).

We forget often that God's ideas about our workload are not the same as our ideas. And they do not include work without his being ultimately over all of it. God knows we need rest in order to refuel, to focus, to gain clarity, to find strength to continue the journey of life, and to connect with other people and fight for the rights of others. If we start from a deficit, we will not be able to bring 100 percent to our community or to fighting injustice.

In 2019, Howard-John Wesley, pastor of the historic Alfred Street Baptist Church in Alexandria, Virginia, shocked the world when he told his congregation that he was stepping away because he was tired. No scandal, no major health issues that were known to the public. In his sermon, he was simply honest about how busy life can be when you are leading in ministry or in any capacity. He said,

> There's a weight a pastor bears in their soul and their emotions that is inescapable. There's not been a day in these past 11 years that I have not woken up and knew that there's something I had to do for the church, that I have to be available for a call, that I journey with people through the highs and the lows of life, through the great moments of celebration and in the valley of death. . . . How many Sundays of four worship services do I have? . . . It leaves me tired. And a nap ain't going to fix it.[2]

Let me ask you something. How has busyness caused you emotional, spiritual, and even physical poverty to the extent that you have been unable to be *present* and to function at 100 percent? Or how often have you heard of some injustice going on in the world only after the verdict had been rendered or the execution had already taken place? Has it ever left you wondering what might have happened had you known sooner or had you had the time in your schedule to participate in the protest or sign that petition?

MAKE A BIGGER IMPACT WITH LESS

After getting checked out by the nurse that day, I ended up in the back of an ambulance getting rushed to a hospital for further examination. Looking back, my calendar was full of great things, but—in all honesty—I wasn't in a good state to be of any help to other people or to a community. I was barely in a position to be good for myself. And it's true that if we have no margin in our lives, we can't take the love of God to the margins of society. After arriving at the hospital and speaking to the physician and my wife, I had to come to grips with the fact that I would need to let go of some things if I wanted to be more effective. I think that the doctor said it best of all: "You've got to say no to the wrong things and say yes to the most important things. Less is more. And less would give you the freedom and the margin needed to impact more people and to build a community."

It was the first time that I started to understand how being busy affected my ability to enter into a state of community with other people or stand with people who wanted me to join in on projects that would influence the community for the better. If we're honest, we'll see that busyness affects every single area of our lives. It affects the way in which we care for ourselves. It affects the ways in which we connect with our loved ones. It hinders us from becoming involved in injustices that need our attention.

Writer and podcaster Emily P. Freeman shares how busyness affects our ability to tackle problems creatively in her book *The Next Right Thing: A Simple, Soulful Practice for Making Life Decisions*. In a chapter titled "Become a Soul Minimalist," she says:

We're letting everyone else's agenda live for free in the sacred space of our creative mind, and it's time for an eviction. This space is necessary for ideas to form, for questions to rise up, for hope to weave her way into our vision for the future, and for the dots of decisions to begin to connect in the quiet places of our mind and heart. Good decisions require creativity, and creativity requires space. This space is necessary for you to speak out against the injustices of the world, the problems you know you can help solve, and the beauty you long to deliver.[3]

Most of us barely allow ourselves time to think, let alone to think creatively. But this problem isn't obvious because it's not like we're filling our calendars with horrible things. At least, the vast majority of us aren't. I was involved with projects that felt necessary and useful, but I desperately needed to reduce my number of commitments so that I could focus more effectively on what mattered most.

As I think about this time in my life, I'm reminded once again of Paul's advice to the church at Corinth as he compared the body's many parts to the members of the church working together collaboratively (see 1 Corinthians 12:12-27). I had been too overwhelmed by activities to help the other members of the body effectively. In some ways, busyness seems to be the opposite—yet equally detrimental cousin—of isolation. We may be "with" people in all of our busyness, but it doesn't necessarily mean we're having the impact that we could have. I was physically *with* my family in the evenings but they surely weren't getting the best of me. And I was physically *with* my students during the day but they weren't getting the best of me either.

Anyone who has ever had to wear a cast to help mend a broken bone can tell you that the most frustrating part of the whole situation is not being able to care for the other parts of their body. But when we are free from the constraints of a cast, we can move again and be effective in service again to those around us while also making time to care for ourselves. Choosing just a few things in our communities in which to be involved allows us to help make the world a better place. Why? Because impact requires focus. I learned later from my stepfather that "the more you narrow your focus, the greater your possible impact."

In December 2018, *Forbes* released an important article titled "Busyness Is Our Worst Addiction." Normally, when we hear the word *addiction*, we think about things like drugs, alcohol, hoarding, or negative things that drive people into destructive cycles and behaviors that ultimately contribute to the formation of unhealthy habits that are hard to break.[4] This article warns us that busyness, when we place great value on it, is also dangerous. Societally, we tend to use busyness as a means of trying to assert self-worth, gain validation, and establish a meaningful way of living.[5]

The truth is that if more people had calendars created with margin in them, we'd be able to come together with other people in deep and meaningful ways, thinking of the issues we could put our hands and feet to. What if less *is* actually more and could help us achieve greater focus and generate a greater positive impact for ourselves and our communities?

HAVE THE COURAGE TO RESET

If you identify with where I was in my twenties, then you have perhaps fallen victim to a culture that has pushed meaningful activity out of the way in favor of busyness and validation. If someone were to ask you right now something as simple as "How are you doing?" and your automatic response was "I'm busy," or "I don't have time to do anything," then chances are that you have started to wear busyness like a badge of honor. You may be filling your schedule to its breaking point with things that, for various reasons, you feel like you "have" to do.

You'd probably agree with me, though, when I say that busyness is a thief. It is, essentially, a criminal that we have allowed to break into our homes and rob our families of joyful memories and of the ability to live with intention. It's the wall that causes divisions and prevents churches from working together in such a way that they might have a greater impact on communities. It's a culprit that steals so many wonderful opportunities away from people who could make a real difference in this world. A lack of any spare energy is the primary reason why so many people are totally unavailable to pursue— and even unaware of—their God-given potential.

I'll never forget the knock at our door a couple of years ago from a friend who had spread himself too thinly. It was December of 2018, the night before Love Beyond Walls was preparing to set up a warming station and mobilize people to care for those experiencing homelessness throughout the holidays. All of a sudden, we heard someone at the door.

That's strange, I thought. *It's almost 10 p.m. Who in the world could be at our door this late?*

I was surprised to see my friend and next-door neighbor, Tim, standing there. I invited him in because it was cold outdoors and he looked like he had something important to share. Tim and his family hadn't really been involved in our organization because he and his wife were almost always working. But I never pressure anyone to get involved with what we are doing; I just really enjoyed his friendship, and our daughters were also close friends.

This night was different, though. After Tim and I sat down at the kitchen table, he said, "I'm sorry, man. I apologize that I haven't been as involved with what your organization does."

"It's not a big deal, my friend. I just enjoy having you as a friend," I replied.

He continued, "Earlier today, I thought about how busy I have been and why I haven't had time to really do anything that is meaningful. I cannot believe I have been so focused on work that I have forgotten what really matters, like family and doing positive things in this world."

"What happened, Tim?" I asked, because this was not like him at all.

"Earlier today, I was driving my family around, doing some shopping, when we came to a stoplight. The light was red, I was distracted, my wife was texting on her phone, the music was blaring, and both my children were in the backseat. Out of the blue, my daughter starts crying."

"Why did she start crying?"

At this point, Tim was almost in tears. "My daughter saw a mother and child standing in the cold, holding a sign that said: 'We are cold and need something to eat, please help.' I didn't see it, my wife didn't see it, but my child did. I guess I have been so busy and distracted that I didn't even notice the woman. That's when I thought about you."

Tim and I continued to talk, and that night he ended up delegating some of his work to other people and canceling some of the hobby-related activities that he had previously scheduled. He even ended some things that he had undertaken repeatedly simply because he felt that he always needed to be doing something! He found the courage to let go in order to free up his schedule for more family time and to get involved in things that his wife and children had been asking him to become involved with for years. The next day, Tim brought his family to serve with us, and I'll never forget what he said to me: "I refuse to be this busy and distracted again in my life. It feels weird not to have anything on the agenda, but this is healthy. I'm here in the community and it feels good to be doing our part."

That's it. Tim had reached the point I had been in during my twenties. And he found the courage to give up the things that mattered least in order to start rebuilding his life around what mattered most: being with people—but not just for the sake of enjoyment. He rebuilt his life for the sake of something more deeply fulfilling: caring for the vulnerable and seeking justice for those who need it.

The courage that Tim finally found is not easy to find. Letting go of certain parts of our identity that we have clung to for years will be difficult. Because let's face it: in most of our minds, our identities are so closely intertwined with our "worth" that it's difficult to separate who we are from what we do. Making the decision to step away from a whirlwind of motion leaves us in a stillness that can be extremely uncomfortable. We're forced to ask who we are then. Are we *enough*? God tells us exactly that we are enough and worthy. The Bible says yes, we are (Psalm 139:13-14).

LET'S MAKE ROOM

Wanting to connect with others and work toward correcting injustice in the world are healthy goals, but before we can really jump into meaningful work out in the world, we have to endeavor to do some hard work *inside*. We've got to reorient our lives and churches and look at some of the ways we have turned to busyness to try to achieve a sense of fulfillment, of being filled up.

Like Martha in the Bible, we've been given a choice—the freedom to choose our priorities—which often means that we neglect what matters most. After my time in the hospital, my wife and I understood that if we were going to continue to undertake good, important work in our community by being present and serving others, then we had to arrange our priorities based on what we wanted to stand for. It was a challenge for me to begin evaluating what was truly important for my life and what wasn't. Sometimes we hold on to things out of habit, and other times we hold on to activities because we're fearful of the unknown. I believe this is why it was so hard for the children of Israel to let go of Egypt. Although Egypt was an oppressive place and threatening to their very existence, it was also a place that they had become extremely comfortable in. This meant that even when God was leading them out of oppression, they were wishing for the comfortable parts of their life in Egypt.

In order to help our family move toward greater health and out of an automatic pilot mode, my wife and I developed a "Let Go List": a list of things that we would either cease immediately or slowly phase ourselves out of in order to embrace activities that aligned with our values. We began the process of leaving behind things we were doing simply to fill dead space and to feel "productive." This list started small and ended up becoming very long. It's essentially the list that forced us to create margin in our lives to free us up to do the things we felt very passionate about doing in the community. Why? Because Jesus spent time being proximate with people and establishing authentic relationships with those whom he cared about, and we wanted to make sure that our lives reflected this value as well.

If you find yourself in a state of constant busyness, I encourage you to begin asking yourself tough questions— questions that will lead you to a place of greater freedom to serve in the ways in which you are uniquely called. Here are a few you can start with:

- What are your values?
- What keeps you from your main goals?
- What have you said yes to that you shouldn't have?
- What activities do you engage in that you'd miss if they were taken away?
- What are some of the things you have been doing that have pulled you away from the things that God has placed on your heart or from being involved in the community like you truly desire?
- If you created your own "Let Go List," what would be on it?

These questions are only the tip of the iceberg in what you may be able to ask yourself to begin letting go of some of the things that could be weighing you down. What would it look like to create a life that allowed you the time to reset, to connect with others, and, as Micah advises us, "to act justly and to love mercy / and to walk humbly with your God" (Micah 6:8 NIV)?

I encourage you to start thinking now about what your own "Let Go List" might look like. I challenge you to stop everything you are doing and write down the things you know you need to let go of. Moving out of busyness and beginning to make the necessary adjustments to your schedule will enable you to move toward a life of freedom and fulfillment within the community.

CHAPTER THREE

PURSUE SOMETHING REAL

It was January 2020, and I had been invited to speak to a group of business, nonprofit, and ministry leaders about what it means to truly see the poor and affirm their dignity by becoming proximate to people who weren't like them. The room was packed, and as I surveyed it, I remember wishing that Mr. Moore could be there to be a part of it. It seemed like the man who had invested so much in the leader I'd become should have been able to be there. I thought of him often as I shared my personal story that day. Passionately recalling the details about how Mr. Moore saw me and encouraged me to overcome my struggles of temporary homelessness as a young man, I also told of how he lived a life of frugality so that he could have the freedom to assist people who were struggling with addiction and poverty. This story served as my illustration about the importance of proximity, and how proximity actually changes us and those whom we seek to serve. I shared the truth that proximity literally changes everything.

After the talk, Paul, a nonprofit leader and attendee, walked up to me and asked if we could grab a coffee. Two days later, we were sitting in a coffee shop together, and he opened up to me and shared his story—a story about giving up the traditional Western pursuit of happiness and then finding it anyway when he pursued something much deeper: justice.

He explained that he had always wanted to give back to those who were experiencing hardship but only from a distance, and in a saviorism way. To that end, he'd decided to go down the route many of us turn to: the idea that one day when he had finally made enough money, he would do something big for his fellow man and make the world a better place. So he worked extremely hard, putting in eighty to a hundred hours per week and routinely sleeping in the warehouse that housed his business. He was working so hard that he was even missing precious hours with his newborn child.

He communicated that he was isolated from his family and friends and busier than he had ever been. And though he might've considered himself productive, life sure didn't feel meaningful. Paul had bought into the notion that success meant working until he had hit a certain level of financial security. Meanwhile, he was missing out on the opportunity to live a truly successful life, one that centered on meaningful moments of connection with others and serving the world in the ways he had always dreamed about. He was living a very empty life in pursuit of something he thought would one day be important for him and his family.

This kind of belief is not uncommon in our Western culture. A typical life trajectory looks something like this: become successful, make a lot of money, and then help others. For many, this seems to be the right order of things. In fact, I've heard highly respected Christian financial gurus advise people to do this very thing: to accumulate wealth, and then live generously. This is regarded as the pursuit of the American dream.

Americans work hard to achieve "success," often sacrificing what will truly bring them joy in favor of money. In essence, we trade one type of poverty for another. We say yes to having healthy bank accounts while saying no to the prospects of enjoying connections and having a sense of belonging, which are the things that make our spirits healthy. The false belief that money is what provides for our ultimate good and safety has resulted in a toxic form of capitalism—one that ignores suffering in order to sustain comfortable lifestyles for the majority. The result is lifestyles that ultimately are found to be emotionally and spiritually unsatisfying and horrifying statistics that add up while we wait for a more perfect time to offer our help.

There are currently over 40.3 million people who are still enslaved around the world.[1] This number includes those in forced labor, those who have been sex-trafficked, and those in a forced marriage. If that weren't enough, the United

States alone is home to over half a million homeless individuals,[2] and had 417 mass shootings in 2019.[3] According to a report released by the Institute for Policy Studies in partnership with the Poor People's Campaign,

> More than 95 million Americans (nearly 30 percent of the total population) are either in poverty or considered "low-income" (below twice the poverty line), using the Official Poverty Measure. That number rises to 43.5% (over 140 million people) when using the Supplemental Poverty Measure (SPM), which takes into account federal assistance resources as well as critical out-of-pocket expenses.[4]

The list of injustices goes on, with staggering statistic after statistic.

Waiting until we're "ready" to enter into restorative work does not honor the humanity in all of us. Instead, it places our individual needs above the needs of those who are in the most danger.

What could happen if we entertained a new version of the American dream wherein we realize that our collective strength helps the individual as well? The answer to this question can be found in the second half of Paul's story when he decided to shift his life's focus from "I" to "we." He understood that to conquer the injustices we see in the world today, he had to see that the world was much bigger than his solo pursuits.

FINDING A NEW WAY TO LIVE

The shift in perspective that Paul experienced arrived in a way that was similar to my own journey. It was an event that shook him to his core and caused him to question whether or not he was living his life according to the right values and priorities.

It caused him to ask himself why he was really working all of those long hours. What kind of positive change was he making? In those moments of questioning himself, he realized that his quest for money was really getting in the way of what he could have been doing to make a difference right then and there. Wanting to honor the memory of his friend who had suddenly passed away, he decided not to wait any longer to pursue a dream that was bigger than a for-profit pursuit and that had been placed in his heart.

So Paul got to work with this new kind of goal in mind. He wanted to build a community of tiny homes for survivors of sex trafficking. But he also felt completely overwhelmed and out of his depth. The only things he knew for sure were that he had enough materials to start framing a house, a team of Christian and non-Christian volunteers—made up of some retired construction workers—to help with the building process itself, and just enough money to build that first house.

Once a bit of progress had been made, the endeavor created a buzz in the community. Soon enough, people began stepping up in ways that Paul could not have imagined. Huge donations were made, labor was volunteered, and tools and materials were purchased by those who saw that this project would allow sex-trafficking survivors to begin to rebuild their lives. The building of these homes galvanized a community of people to work together in order to bring about a huge change in the lives of those who needed justice.

WHAT'S *ACTUALLY* GOOD FOR US

Paul's story is an example of a simple truth about entering into a community for the purposes of justice and connection: it is really what's best for all involved. It brings needed restoration to those we aspire to help and it breathes life into our own spiritual development. Yet instead, we work for years distracted by the false idea that increasing our wealth will improve our own overall well-being. Certainly, our Western culture has propagated this idea for years; the mentality of "looking out for number one" is ingrained in us all. Our culture promotes being focused on self-gratification, to always put yourself first and allow others to take a back seat. Jesus modeled a different way of being. The Bible says that Jesus came to give and even challenges others to live this way. Jesus commands us to include our neighbors in the way that we love. The Bible doesn't say love yourself as you love yourself. It commands us to share this love with others around us by not making our lives and love only about us.

The majority of us live very separate lives from each other, seeking the fulfillment of our own goals. One of the results of this can be the erosion of compassion. We bypass the man or woman who is experiencing homelessness on our way inside the grocery store and rationalize to ourselves that groceries for our own family must come first— even though, more often than not, buying just a few more items is not going to break anyone's bank. Nor would taking the time to actually see that person and to have even just a few minutes of conversation with them.

Ironically, while we live in isolation, our real desire is to be in relationship with others, and so we settle for "likes" on social media, or the occasional comments that make us feel better about not truly connecting with others. We feast upon the empty validation that they bring, forgoing something real—like community, connection, and joining the fight for justice.

FINDING PURPOSE

What if we didn't have to live this way? What if we intentionally opted out of the culture of busyness and adopted a lifestyle that placed spiritual and relational wealth above the pursuit of monetary wealth? What if this type of prioritizing caused us to pursue a life of deeper spiritual purpose? What if we could start to make a huge effect now? I believe that our lives would be much richer. No—not materially, but spiritually and socially. We could have lives that are rich in meaningful connections and important work that has been undertaken in the name of humanity, having afforded ourselves with the necessary margin to do something about injustice. In the Netflix documentary film *Minimalism*, economist and sociologist Juliet Schor says:

> The American Dream has a long history that started out as a concept that was really more about opportunity. The US is a land of opportunity where somebody can start out at the bottom, work hard, and do well. There's no question that what it means to have made it or to have achieved the American Dream in the United States has increased tremendously in material terms. One-hundred-thousand-dollar-a-year-plus kind of income became more and more an aspirational norm across the society, because that's what's portrayed as normal on TV, a six-figure income.[5]

And while many Americans aren't striving for the six figures they see exemplified on TV and are simply working to pay the bills or living paycheck to paycheck, the truth remains that we live in a constant state of pressure to strive and make something out of nothing. Right now, there are millions of Americans working forty to sixty hours a week carrying the stress of not making enough to keep their heads and families above water. People have a deep desire to find support from the surrounding community, but the hustle and bustle of life and the pressure to make ends meet for ourselves and our families seem to pull us away. The scales of Western justice are weighted heavily toward fueling our own prosperity and the prosperity of those who live within our four walls.

Sometimes it seems we've forgotten that God specializes in using those things that are deemed least likely and foolish to not only bring about change in their part of the world but also create broader social change. He doesn't require CEO status or seven digits in a bank account before you are qualified to make a difference in the world. No one's money would have been on David to win a fight with the giant named Goliath. No one would have predicted that a young Jewish girl named Esther would save her nation by leveraging the power in her voice and stance. But that is the way God writes stories! God uses whomever he chooses to fulfill the purpose of bringing justice to the world. He will use whoever is willing, regardless of their economic standing.

As a businessman, Paul had resources, but far more important was the change of heart that Paul had about what to do with those resources. Undoubtedly, he would have continued to live "successfully" by the world's standards—but at what cost to him spiritually? He would have forever lost that time with his child and would have robbed himself of an opportunity for deep, satisfying work that blessed a group of women in profound ways.

And let's not forget about all of the people who served alongside Paul. This project brought a group of people together who had an opportunity to experience what it was like to make an impact for the greater good. Each of them forged new relationships and leaned into what they were created to do by using their skills and providing resources, time, and money. Joy and fulfillment were brought to the community, and dignity was restored to the women who, having been through so much, now at least have homes that they can call their own. This is what can be accomplished when we take the step to move away from an "I" mindset and embrace a mindset that says "when *we* stand," beautiful things can and will happen. God tends to bring those who will be blessed by the process into partnership with us.

For Paul, as for anyone, the decision to take the leap of faith that was necessary to even begin this project was not an easy one. Nor was the path to success a smooth or linear one. A conversation with one person led to a conversation with another person that needed to happen; one detail needed to come through before another could. The path was not always clear, to say the least. But that is almost always what a true walk of faith looks like. We can't always see a clear way to a solution. And yet, by the power of *we*, everything came together for the greater good. And there is no doubt that Paul changed his life—and the lives of others—for the better.

An article titled "The Secret to Happiness Is Helping Others" asks whether the "truism" of "it is better to give than to receive" does actually have any truth in it. As it turns out, there's science to back the claim up: "Scientific research provides compelling data to support the anecdotal evidence that giving is a powerful pathway to personal growth and lasting happiness." The article elaborates:

Through fMRI technology, we now know that giving activates the same parts of the brain that are stimulated by food and sex. Experiments show evidence that altruism is hardwired in the brain—and it's pleasurable. Helping others may just be the secret to living a life that is not only happier but also healthier, wealthier, more productive, and meaningful.[6]

Statements like this make it sound as if we're hardwired to serve and that, if we are not embedding opportunities in our own lives to do so, then we're missing out on something that brings us a fundamental level of joy and meaning. And yet, in society as a whole, we consider serving, volunteering, giving, and taking the time to form and sustain meaningful connections to be "extras" in the busy schedules of our lives. We make little to no time for these things that truly matter.

Joshua Becker, author and founder of the blog *Becoming Minimalist*, recounts the story of how his journey with the philosophy of minimalism began. His young son simply wanted to play catch with him one afternoon, but Becker—being too busy with things that needed doing around the house, like cleaning out the garage—didn't have the time. As the day wore on, he began to become more and more frustrated by how much stuff there was in the garage to clean and sort. And what for? Becker explains it in this way:

I remember looking at the pile of possessions in my driveway—dusty old things [that] I'd spent all day cleaning and organizing. While looking at the pile, out of the corner of my eye, I caught a glimpse of my son swinging alone on the swing set in the backyard. And suddenly I realized, my possessions were not making me happy. But even worse, they were distracting me from the very thing that did bring me happiness. I had wasted my time and my energy on things that didn't matter. As a result, I missed spending time and energy on the things that do.[7]

It seems obvious that the quest for more money and more stuff does not make us happy. We see it with celebrities and athletes who get to the very top of their game and have every possible luxury at their fingertips yet struggle with depression or drug addiction. Tragically, there are those who have even taken their own lives, like Robin Williams and Chester Bennington. An excess of money and things is not the answer to our quest for meaning. It is not until we are spiritually well that we will lead lives that feel meaningful. So many of us, though, live in spiritual poverty.

Spiritual poverty is not a lack of food or material resources but rather a lack of connection with those around us, a lack of belonging and acceptance, and a lack of a relationship with God. It is the kind of poverty that we have all felt at one point or another in our lives, and it is this kind of wealth that we open ourselves up to when we decide to enter into a community.

So how do we free ourselves from our financial and material concerns to make space for more meaningful connections? The answer is really twofold: we quit allowing the quest for financial security to be our main decision-maker, and we begin streamlining our lives, ridding ourselves of the kinds of distractions that get in the way of us finding our passion for serving.

DOWNSIZE IF NECESSARY

Wanting to have things like a nice house in a good neighborhood with plenty of money to spare, when everyone around you has those things, is a natural response. But why do we believe that achieving material things will make our lives better? What if the American dream only serves as a form of distraction to keep us from living a life of intentionality for God?

My friends Carl and Jennifer have worked hard throughout their whole lives, and they consequently achieved success in accordance with most definitions in our culture. They were living the American dream, complete with a big, beautiful home in a lovely neighborhood. Yet, despite how much they had accomplished, they did not feel content with just enjoying the lifestyle that they had established for themselves.

Carl and Jennifer were believers and sought out intentional ways to live for God. They realized that God was calling them to provide a loving and stable family for kids in the foster care system. They felt compelled to help kids who, through no fault of their own, were unable to live safely with their families and needed the love, acceptance, and stability of a healthy family while their parents worked to better their own homes and situations.

My friends' house was really nice, and they did have some extra space, but they felt that it was not enough for what they were feeling called to. They knew they had the means to do more, and they sensed that God wanted them to host more kids than what their current home could accommodate.

One of the greatest needs in the foster system is for people who can take in siblings so that they do not have to be separated into different foster homes. When kids have already lost everything else in their lives, the experience of being separated from their siblings is devastating. There is also a great need for space for older youth. So many things in these kids' lives are uncertain and unstable, and they often have little that they can call their own. For older kids especially, it can be very healthy to have their own space—a place where they can feel in control of their environment and have privacy to process their emotions and to take some time away from everything else that is going on around them.

Carl and Jennifer decided to sell their house in order to buy one that was less "nice" but better-suited to welcoming larger numbers of children. Their new home did not have the same luxuries and was not situated in the prized neighborhood of their previous house, but it gave them the space to take in siblings and to provide older kids with some privacy.

This family took a big step back in terms of their social status. In a culture that is so driven by "doing better" than others in various ways and being the first to upgrade, it can be really hard to downgrade one's material possessions. And although my friends would have been doing more than enough in the eyes of the world to host one or two kids in their original house, they were not satisfied with fitting foster care into their current circumstances. Instead, they defied cultural pressures and pursued new circumstances that provide a better space for children—a home where they are accepted and belong.

LEAVE YOUR COMFORT ZONE BEHIND

You may not feel a call to sell your home or move out of your current neighborhood—but you may be able to "downgrade" in some other area of your life so that you can better help the people whom you feel called to help.

Ask yourself whether your family can drive a used car as opposed to a new car. This might help free up money that would ordinarily be used for a monthly car payment. You might also consider using more coupons at the grocery store, eating meals in your home more often instead of going out, reducing your cellphone bill, opting into a streaming service as opposed to traditional cable TV, and buying clothes secondhand to free up income to be directed toward a cause. These are just a few ways that we can all practically increase our financial resources in order to give to organizations that are doing meaningful work in our communities or help fund areas of service that we are passionate about.

I'm not saying that having nice things or upgrades are bad things in themselves. Sometimes, though, we have to give up things that are good because they are getting in the way of following God's call or the search for justice to which we could contribute—and which could be far better and more rewarding. I encourage you to look at all of the things in your life and to assess them, weigh them, and wrestle with them to see if they help you to serve and become proximate to those who are around you, or take up unwanted and unnecessary space in your life. Identifying these things means that your life could look very different than it does now and that what is "best" may not adhere to the values, expectations, or lifestyles of everyone around you.

My challenge to you is to reevaluate your core values as an individual or as a leader, whether in the context of your home or your organization. If you find that the framework you make your daily decisions in is founded on what will give you financial security but does not afford space to connect with others or bring light into the world through justice work, find the courage to take some big steps toward the freedom for which you have been longing.

If you desire to make a strong impact in and on this world, then some tough decisions will need to be made to create more space in your life so you can be available in ways that can truly bring God glory in the world around you. Make them—and dare to refuse to look back.

CHAPTER FOUR

BE BRAVE
AND UNLEARN

N ot too long ago, my daughter was very excited at the prospect of a little girl who looked very much like her—who had dark skin—playing the titular role of Ariel in the remake of *The Little Mermaid* movie. What I remember most of all, though, is my daughter's subsequent sadness when she saw hashtags like #NotMyAriel on social media sites, along with other racist comments. Hateful sentiments from individuals who asserted that Ariel needed to be "a cute girl with white skin" were all too readily available for my young daughter to read online. I recall that she repeatedly asked me "Why?" throughout the entirety of the next day, having read many of these comments. I tried to educate her by drawing on both historical examples and my own experiences—ones that I, sadly, suffer weekly. These are experiences that none of my White counterparts have had to document or try to explain to their children. Not one. This is in part because Black children encounter the topic of race at earlier ages than White children. The *Washington Post* reported that "black families can't afford to wait until adolescence to begin conversations about identity, and most black children, by age 10, have an adult view of biological and social racial constructs."[1]

As a Black man though, incapable of shedding the skin into which I was born, I know that I don't have the privilege of shying away from difficult conversations about the cultural assumptions of Black inferiority that America's history of discrimination has caused. I'm reminded nearly every day that other people in the country of my birth see me as being inferior. I'm reminded when people intentionally cross to the other side of the street when I'm walking down the same sidewalk. I'm reminded every time that I'm in a predominantly White space and have to prove my intelligence, or when a White woman clutches her purse when I walk in her direction. I've been reminded when I've participated in events as a nonprofit leader and have been mistaken for the janitor simply because I happen to be the only Black person in a group of White leaders.

PAY ATTENTION TO THE STORIES OF THE MARGINALIZED

My stories are not unique, nor are my experiences of coming from a minority culture. My story is common to those who exist on the margins—those who have gone unseen and been disregarded because they have not mattered enough to people who believe that being poor means that you are somehow less human and unworthy of the same love that we all seek. However, as everyone across the world reaches out for one another in a new climate of enforced physical distancing due to Covid-19, the cracks in our systems of care—the symptoms of our failure to care—are painfully evident for all to see, from people experiencing homelessness who find themselves without access to sinks in which to wash their hands and help protect themselves from the virus to the disproportionate impact that Covid-19 has had on Black communities. We must ask ourselves, what will it take to bring about lasting change? True change will happen only when we can bravely begin to unlearn harmful attitudes that lead to injustice.

The changes I'm referring to are less about behavioral changes and more about improving the ways in which we view and understand people. They are not about adding tokenistic "acts of service" to our schedules but rather something that goes much deeper. They involve a change of heart: one that begs us to let go of believing that we're superior to others in any way and to start confronting the ways in which we've previously ostracized people due to the color of their skin, which side of the border they find themselves on, or the amount of money that they have in their bank accounts. And that is just on a personal level—because, at the same time, our governments are going to have to start becoming accountable for the policies that they have enacted over the years: policies that were intended to keep entire races of people separate, marginalized, feeling inferior, and pushed to the fringes of society. This kind of unlearning forces us to confront things about ourselves that are unattractive. The word *racism*, for example, can often not even be uttered for fear that it will immediately shut down communication between the speaker and the hearer. The suggestion that someone might in fact be a racist or promote racist ideas by their inaction—personally, politically, or both—can stir feelings of intense personal shame which can lead to all-out denial for that person. This denial in turn adds to the racial trauma that a person of color has already experienced. On the other hand, when a person of the majority culture can acknowledge their own potential bias, listen without defensiveness, become educated on the experiences of people of color, and begin to take actions that bring equity to a community that is not their own—this is extremely powerful. Recognizing the humanity in all and the inherent image of God in all is restorative work. But it takes an acknowledgment that we are not all—as of yet—treated the same. And we have not all—yet—engaged in the work of eliminating that reality.

LEARNING HOW THE PAST SHAPES US

The unlearning that needed to happen for my wife and me came as a result of a life-altering experience. When our son was only two years old, he suffered a major health scare in the form of a seizure during an otherwise normal morning at daycare. I'll never forget hearing my wife's voice that day over the phone, telling me that I needed to get to the daycare center, nor will I ever forget the panic that I felt. It was the most scared that I'd ever been in my life, seeing my son lying unconscious on the floor, surrounded by first responders. Although my son survived the incident, it changed our family forever. It's the type of parental pain you cannot explain; there are only tears and unanswered questions.

Both my wife and I had experienced different levels of trauma ourselves while growing up. It was the seriousness of what we were dealing with in terms of our son's condition, though, that ultimately forced us to make some commitments in the hospital room that day. We both made a commitment to being healthier for each other, for our son, and for the community that we were serving through our organization.

The essence of what's truly inside us comes out during times of challenge. Knowing how my upbringing has shaped me has helped me to be a better leader in my family and in the community. I have had to learn how certain experiences in my present life may trigger the memories of things that I went through in my childhood. For example, I vividly remember experiencing a lack of communication and affection when I was a child, coupled with high levels of anger and various situations that left me feeling isolated and unwanted. I know that challenges and hardships in my adult life can evoke those same emotions in me, and I am aware of how hard I have to work to manage them when such challenges arise. To speak truthfully, if I am not doing the real work internally, then I will not be any good for anyone.

My wife's upbringing wasn't much better. She was raised by her single mother and watched her father struggle with drug addiction and with being in and out of prison. We both understand that we are all flawed; both of us have come from circumstances in which we have had to fight extra hard to overcome adversity and to change things for our family and for the communities that we serve.

No matter where we come from, it's up to us to recognize how the past has potentially taught us some unhealthy ways of thinking. If we understand how our history has shaped us, it will help us avoid perpetuating the same hurts that we have experienced ourselves with our loved ones and in our communities. It's true that isolation and busyness can keep us from connecting. Yet perhaps what's even more detrimental is when we allow past hurts, pains, and traumas to prevent us from connecting with people and from working and taking a stand together. Sometimes, the greatest barrier for a person, church, or group of people who all want to make a difference or to engage in justice work is not related to their level of willingness but rather in how the past has shaped their reactions to the present moment. If it is true that while on an airplane you should first put on your own oxygen mask in the case of an emergency before you help the passenger next to you, it could also be true when it comes to engaging in causes and issues that could possibly stir up difficult feelings and emotions with which we haven't yet dealt on an individual level.

I am in no way saying that we need to be perfect before we are able to meaningfully engage in the justice work that we feel called to undertake. What I *am* saying is that we need to be honest about the things that might prevent us from giving our very best. In fact, it is important to remember that God always uses imperfect people to accomplish God's will. I also believe that what Henri Nouwen communicates in his book *The Wounded Healer* is true: "The great illusion of leadership is to think that man can be led out of the desert by someone who has never been there. Our lives are filled with examples which tell us that leadership asks for understanding and that understanding requires sharing."[2] In essence, Nouwen is speaking to the fact that we are not perfect, and that we all have been wounded, but that shouldn't stop or hinder us from engaging with others. As a matter of fact, the person that is able to relate most to someone who is suffering is someone who has also suffered. God uses imperfect people to create hope in the world every single day. In fact, your imperfections qualify you even more if you are open enough to embrace them.

The process of engaging in any type of justice work or forming connections with other people will almost always require that you undertake some type of internal work in order to rid yourself of discriminatory feelings. Internal work also helps you become healthy enough to develop healthy relationships or to make an impact in a specific area. In fact, the more proximate you get to other people, the more you find out what is truly in your heart.

I remember a particular occasion when a middle-aged White woman volunteered at our center in College Park, Georgia. It was around the time of the July 2016 shooting of Philando Castile, who was fatally shot by a police officer during a traffic stop while reaching for his wallet. After serving, a group of volunteers started talking about these recent events. This middle-aged White lady was offended by the conversation and began saying disrespectful things to others in the room. Later we discovered that her father had been a police officer who was killed in the line of duty in a car accident. Nobody knew this at the time, however; I only found out because I asked her to step aside to talk through her feelings with me. Though the woman was in an entirely different set of circumstances than her father had been in, the conversation itself triggered something in her in that moment that made her yell at others, thereby disconnecting her from the people around her.

She ended up telling me that she had delayed dealing with it. I imagine that there are many others out there who have also put off dealing with past traumas and that what's resulted is an inability to work effectively and truly connect with people. One of my mentors phrased it this way: "God is more concerned with the work that God is doing inside of you than with what you can offer the world." I think part of that is true. If our goal is to connect with others in a way that addresses injustice and brings healing and hope to the world, then we must also be willing to do that same work on the inside.

We have all seen how the avoidance of internal work can be passed along to others in unhealthy ways or even replicated. We know what happens when internal issues go unaddressed. We've seen this play out in churches when they continue to hurt people because of unhealthy practices in leadership and in organizations when they perpetuate cycles of dysfunction because of how their history has shaped them. We have also seen this fleshed out in families when parents abuse their children and spouses because they were abused as children—or when they withhold the words "I love you" from their children because it was never said to them in their own households.

Growing up, I found it extremely difficult to connect with my own family. When I came to faith in the Lord, I was an outcast. And some of the men in my family specifically thought I had chosen a path of weakness. They stayed as far away from me as possible and talked negatively behind my back. Not surprisingly, without a firm foundation to draw upon, being a part of any community was initially challenging for me. I didn't understand what it really meant to be part of a group and receive love. Our upbringings can leave wounds, and we must tend to those wounds in order to serve others at our best.

The healing work that we undertake within ourselves is God-honoring. And it often requires a tremendous amount of courage and a willingness to head in a different direction altogether.

FIND A NEW WAY

My friend Matt came face to face with his own need to walk in a different direction back in 2003 while completing an assignment in his clinical psychology course. The course was focused on educating graduate-level students on diverse cultural perspectives so that they might be sensitive to paradigms that were not their own while counseling. As a White man, Matt remembers how one essay assignment left him feeling defensive, as if he were to blame for the problems that Black and Brown people were experiencing. The questions seemed to insinuate that his color gave him a level of privilege that he not only felt frustrated by but quite frankly did not believe actually existed. Matt explains,

At the time I was twenty-two and I looked at the issue really simplistically. I loved everyone and I hadn't done anything to personally cause problems. I felt like I was being coaxed into admitting something that I had not actually done. But the exercise was designed to get you to step out of your own shoes and realize that other people experienced the world differently.

Though he remembers feeling extremely uncomfortable, Matt credits this assignment with being the first step in shifting the way he thought about race. And the second step came as the result of the classroom discussion that followed. The group of students was made up of mostly White and Black people with one Brown person and a

Black professor. As people began to vulnerably share their stories, Matt realized that the privilege that was being insinuated by the essay questions was not a faulty idea but a reality. Many of the students had experienced negative interactions based on race, while he, for the most part, had not.

What's more is that the stories were not those of random people on the internet whom he would never meet but rather real people whom he considered friends. Their stories and their lives became something that propelled him toward new ways of thinking. For example, he could no longer take the overly simplistic view of incidents of police brutality—such as saying, "Well, they must've mouthed off in order to have that kind of thing happen"— but would have to be open to the fact that very often, White and Black people were simply treated differently based solely on the color of their skin.

I remember having a conversation with Matt in which we talked about the differences in our interactions with law enforcement as a White man (him) and a Black man (me). He mentioned the anxiety that he felt when he was pulled over for a traffic violation, specifically anxiety related to the possibility of spending a day in court and away from work, or having his car insurance rates potentially increase. When I pointed out that my anxiety resided in the question of whether I would make it out of the interaction alive, it once again placed things in a new perspective. I told him, "I'm a grown man with degrees from college and I'm working on a PhD. But even to this day if I am pulled over, I place my hands out of the window because I fear for my life and have no idea if my face will be the one on TV with a hashtag to follow."

Hearing stories from and building relationships with those who do not look like him has been the catalyst for most of Matt's major shifts in perspective. And these shifts have led to his decision to have intentional conversations with those he loves who choose not to see their own privilege. He prefers conversations in person, as engaging in social media debate has led to a loss of influence in certain cases, with people just becoming more firmly entrenched in their own ideas. "As long as we can't get in a room with somebody that's different from us, we're in bad shape," he says.

Matt went through the difficult process of being honest with himself about the fact that the way he previously regarded something was incorrect. And because he had the courage to walk in a new direction, he is able to help others do the same. But the change we must first make within ourselves at times seems less voluntary and more essential for moving forward. I think back to that fateful day in my son's hospital room with my wife, or to Paul's story, and I recognize that for each of us the shift in our perspectives came out of experiences that fundamentally changed the way we needed to operate.

One science writer has likened shifts in perspective to the shifts natural states of matter make:

That sudden shift is the physics equivalent of a Saul on the road to Damascus moment, and frankly, such clear-cut transformative moments are rare. But there's more than one kind of phase transition. What I described [is] a first-order transition, which occurs abruptly, such as boiling water or melting ice. A second order phase transition occurs more smoothly and continuously, such as when ferromagnetism switches to paramagnetism in metals like iron, nickel and cobalt, or when a substance becomes superconductive. That strikes me as a better analogy for how we change our minds.[3]

Whether immediate or slowly and over time, though, we have to do the work of change—shifting our mentality to a new perspective—which means that we have to break old thought patterns. This is hard for any of us who have become used to operating in a certain way, especially when we have to make changes that are in opposition to the values and habits that we have formed as a result of our own personal history. However, it can be done, and it not only helps you grow but it also puts you in a position whereby you can connect with people in more meaningful ways.

One of the most challenging issues that we see in the present day is the issue of racism. It's sad to say that we are still dealing with racism in the 2020s because people refuse to be honest about how their history has shaped the way they behave toward people who are of a different hue. To this day, when I speak up about race, I get hate mail from White Christians and pastors, and even death threats from people who are unwilling to deal with their "confirmation bias" or imbedded beliefs.

If we desire to connect with people more fully, we must commit ourselves to undertaking the necessary internal work and being open to going in a new direction altogether. To start with, we must be willing to identify what needs to change. As I write this, I think about the number of people, churches, and organizations who would have a more profound impact if they undertook some difficult internal work and challenged the behaviors that aren't helping them create the life that they want to live within their families or communities—and that could be holding them back from living out the Great Commission that Jesus gave us.

EMBRACE A NEW NORMAL

Whatever false beliefs have been making their way into our psyches since our childhoods must be weeded out in favor of new, inclusive beliefs. Again, we must challenge any view that supports the illusion that we are somehow elite, which is the main, misguided belief that has hindered or stopped us from stepping in to help wherever and whenever we've been needed. Without changing our perspectives, and as long as we think that we're somehow "better" than others, we will continue to disregard the homeless and those who live on the "wrong" side of town, or the person who lives in a different zip code than we do. This kind of thinking goes directly against the teachings of Jesus, who calls us to flip everything that we know on its head.

When I think of the section of Scripture that is known as the Beatitudes, I'm reminded of just how countercultural Jesus' life really was. He did not care about a person's station in life but instead talked openly about how the "weak things" of the world were of vast importance in God's perspective. In Matthew 5:3-12 (ESV), in his Sermon on the Mount, we hear Jesus say:

> Blessed are the poor in spirit, for theirs is the kingdom of heaven.
>
> Blessed are those who mourn, for they shall be comforted.
>
> Blessed are the meek, for they shall inherit the earth.
>
> Blessed are those who hunger and thirst for righteousness, for they shall be satisfied.
>
> Blessed are the merciful, for they shall receive mercy.
>
> Blessed are the pure in heart, for they shall see God.
>
> Blessed are the peacemakers, for they shall be called sons of God.
>
> Blessed are those who are persecuted for righteousness' sake, for theirs is the kingdom of heaven.
>
> Blessed are you when others revile you and persecute you and utter all kinds of evil against you falsely on my account. Rejoice and be glad, for your reward is great in heaven, for so they persecuted the prophets who were before you.

It is notable that, in these lines, Jesus does not say, "Blessed are those who only value people like themselves or care for themselves" or "Blessed are those who seek riches for themselves." On the contrary, he points over and over again to the way in which God affords special favor to those whom we would probably consider to be unfortunate or even cursed. Jesus calls those very same people blessed. The only way we can see each other in the way that God calls us to see each other—in light of the dignity that he gives to us all—is to confront the false narrative of superiority and have the courage to invert it completely.

To do so, we need to adopt an inclusive kind of living —one that invites people of all colors and economic statuses into the conversation, and asks them who they are and what they think. Jesus' way calls for us all to undertake a radical rethink. Only when Jesus' way of thinking—that everyone is worthy of our care—becomes the new normal will we be able to move forward from this moment in history that contains a global pandemic and a growing racial divide and say that we're better for it. What a waste it would be not to learn from this historical season. What a waste it would be just to call this a "difficult time" that we went through without seizing it as a moment for change.

The process of learning from this crisis will require real effort from everyone. And it means that the people who would call themselves "Christians" can no longer rest on church attendance as a measure of their faithfulness to the call of God. A relationship with God must supersede our social contexts; we must begin to look more and more like Jesus in our behaviors and values in our day-to-day lives. This requires that we put our hands and feet to use within our communities, which need not only bring the message of hope that Jesus offers but his provision too. This is not the first time that people both inside and outside church congregations have found it difficult to get food into their homes or have been out of work. These things have been happening for centuries, and in neighborhoods that are close to all of us.

I dare you to pause right now and commit. Commit to changing the direction of your life or the direction of the organization that you are leading. You have the power, right now, to commit to unlearning unhealthy ways so that you can set the tone, from this day forward, for what you will do differently—both in yourself and in the context of an organization.

So what do you need to change? What patterns, ways, and behaviors do you see in yourself or your organization that you wish were different? Have you been closing yourself off to people? Have you not really been trusting new leaders in your organization? Have you been angry toward others because of what has happened to you in the past?

Perhaps there are racist, sexist, or prejudiced ideas that need to be confronted within you or within your organization. If this is the case, a commitment to learning from

those whose skin color and gender are different from yours is paramount. Let me be clear, though, that even if these are not issues for you, it is key that you expose yourself to content from those who differ from you racially, culturally, politically, and in gender. If we read or listen to only those whose opinions match ours, all we're doing is participating in confirmation bias and receiving a mental and emotional pat on the back for being "right."

Additionally, we should ask ourselves what unconfessed or hidden struggles we might still be holding on to. Our unhealthy habits and ways of being can keep us unavailable for God's use and can keep us from seeing how our contributions combined with others' contributions can have an impact on those who need it. One of the first steps you can take to begin to face your secret struggles is to start making a list of them and then find a safe space in which to talk through them—perhaps with a counselor, or with your spouse, or with a leader in your organization. The Bible teaches us that there is power in confession and even more power in prayer.

Sometimes we cannot move forward until we have gone back—until we open up to talk about what we've been through in the past. You may be wrestling with the idea of involving yourself in any type of community because you've been hurt by people who made you feel unworthy or not valued within a particular group. Remember that you are made in God's image and, as such, have inherent value. Healing from the wrongs done to us or that we have done to others can take time, but healing is necessary for our own peace and for our role in restoring dignity and peace to others. If God wants you to unlearn habits so that he might use you to your highest capacity to serve the world, what would you be willing to change?

CHAPTER FIVE

THINK "WE"—NOT "ME"

Until recently the most popular social media memes have been mostly self-seeking. You know the ones. They encourage us to "live our best life" and "hustle hard," and they advise the scroller to "do you." However, I see a subtle shift recently in the form of social media calls to action by some who would rather leverage their platform for meaningful change in the world. Hashtags such as "#ICantBreathe," "#SayHerName," and #RunWithMaud are showing a different kind of America—one that is beginning to wake up to the longstanding injustice that has been perpetrated against Black people in this country and has even caused major brands to publicly say #BlackLivesMatter.

Perhaps due in part to a global pandemic and quarantine orders, people are paying attention to the lives of others. All of our lives have been interrupted long enough to stop and see what Rev. Dr. Martin Luther King Jr. referred to as "the other America" in his 1967 speech of the same name. In it, King contrasts the millions of young people who grow up "in the sunlight of opportunity" with another America, where "millions of work-starved men walk the streets daily in search for jobs that do not exist."[1]

And don't we help contribute to this "other America" when we live in bubbles? When we isolate ourselves from the needs of others, not seeing the plight of persons of color or some of our LGBTQ+ brothers and sisters who are violently murdered from hatred? Or when we advocate against sheltering the homeless in our own neighborhoods because we're afraid they might negatively affect our way of life? As Christians, a life of insulation is the opposite of our calling. Our lives should routinely include stepping into community as servants and seekers of justice.

The historical view of Christianity calls humans to love God and to love their neighbors like they love themselves. The historical life of Jesus clearly exemplified these principles. He spent his adult life on a mission to help people, heal people, and lift them out of their despair. There is an inherent giving up of selfhood and decentering in a life that is lived in such a way. In order to love anyone well, we must first see them and be willing to acknowledge their needs, even if our acknowledgment means that we must give something up of our "self." This might require a willingness to admit privilege and, in doing so, contribute to the increased equity of someone whose inequity has allowed you to financially and socially benefit. It might also mean admitting that you have wielded certain privilege not for the good of your fellow brothers and sisters but for your own personal gain. We must normalize the act of paying attention to the times when our privileges have sheltered us from the realities other people have to suffer through. Power and privilege can be blinding and keep us from seeing clearly what we should be concerned with.

Imagine if the Pharisees had been willing to look at their privilege. What would have happened if they had been willing to step out of their positions of power long enough to really see the people of Israel as opposed to questioning Jesus' reasons for associating with them? We'll never know the answer, of course, but it's easy to see ourselves in the Pharisees' questions, which often had more to do with maintaining their own status and keeping people oppressed than actually trying to minister to them. In the book of John, for example, after Jesus heals a man who's been blind since birth, the Pharisees' first reaction is not to rejoice at the restoration, but to discredit the miracle worker, the man who's been healed, and his family.

> Some of the Pharisees said, "This man is not from God, for he does not observe the sabbath." But others said, "How can a man who is a sinner perform such signs?" And they were divided. So they said again to the blind man, "What do you say about him? It was your eyes he opened." He said, "He is a prophet."
>
> The Jews did not believe that he had been blind and had received his sight until they called the parents of the man who had received his sight and asked them, "Is this your son, who you say was born blind? How then does he now see?" (John 9:16-19)

According to Jewish history, "the Pharisees were pri-
marily not a political party but a society of scholars and
pietists. They enjoyed a large popular following, and in the
New Testament they appear as spokesmen for the majority
of the population."[2] If they could prove that the healing
was not real, then they could retain their status as power
holders of information and not worry about doing anything new. Life would remain tilted in their favor.

The Pharisees' top priority was looking out for their own
desires and perceived needs. Serving requires not only the
gift of time but also the gift of seeing beyond our own
needs. We may not be affected negatively by certain government policies, but someone we would call a brother or
sister in Christ could be. For example, Covid-19 spreading
like wildfire within the confines of a prison or underneath
a bridge where many people are living might not affect you,
but the woman in the pew next to yours may have a brother
serving twenty years in that prison, and it matters greatly
to her. When she asks you not only to pray but to dial the
governor on your phone and ask him to do something
about the problem, the situation is not political to her but
rather an issue of personhood and dignity. You may desire
to get into a debate with her instead, asking her to defend
her position, but would this really be what Jesus would ask
of us? Or would he ask us to show this woman compassion?
It takes more work to discredit her opinion on the matter
than to send an email or pick up the phone. Let us not
present hoops to discredit others just so we can disengage

and disown our own responsibility as a fellow brother or sister in Christ.

Loving one another in the way God calls us to must also mean a willingness to hear worldviews that are different than our own, and to listen to them with compassion and empathy. When we deny our community the respect of listening, a willingness to change, and the offering of our time, expertise, and finances in ways that could benefit us all, we're also denying our community the ability to tackle the social injustices that are most pressing. When we assume a posture of being willing to link arms instead of cross them, we can build healthy relationships and communities. Another word for this helpful posture is *humility*. Most of us struggle with its opposite: pride.

LAYING PRIDE ASIDE

Pastor Erik Raymond has called out the growing problem of pride within church leadership, pointing to the rise of the celebrity pastor and cautioning leaders to beware of their real motives. "It is not the acquisition of popularity that is the problem," he writes, "but rather the prideful aspiration of it."[3]

At the root of any number of unhealthy habits that hinder our ability to collaborate successfully—both in the home and in the organizations that we serve—is pride. It gives rise to stubbornness that blocks our willingness to compromise and prevents us from hearing criticism that may lead to our growth, thereby allowing thoughts of superiority to fester. At its most treacherous, over-whelming pride and superiority can lead to some of our most heinous social injustices, like racism.

I'm reminded of an experience that I once had as an African American pastor on staff at a predominantly White church. The feelings of superiority and bigotry that existed within its ranks took very little time to surface. I remember being at a staff party where I was about to be introduced to the rest of the staff for the first time. Another staff member climbed up on stage and introduced me as their first "token." My heart dropped. I was deeply offended and wanted to storm out of that room in protest. That same woman went on to describe me as "colored" to over a hundred staff members. But this group of leaders were claiming that they were all about diversity, and would not listen to my feedback when I told them how racist it was to introduce me that way. A collaborative heart will invite not just surface-level diversity but true inclusion—and they are not the same. While diversity invites people to the table, inclusion empowers them to be heard while at that table. Diversity without inclusion is shallow marketing. I do not wish to sit at any tables that want my skin for marketing but not my voice for truth and perspective.

Their pride not only cut our ties, but it was also hard for many other African Americans to stay there and worship as well. I still remember the sting I felt when I heard those words and the dead silence that persisted right afterward. Nobody spoke up.

To some people reading this, I'm sure this sounds crazy. You're wondering how someone in our modern culture could even imagine saying these things, let alone actually say them into a microphone in public. But the truth is that these were just words, and the beliefs that underpinned those words are the ones that are currently keeping people in poverty and oppressed by systems that do not allow them to gain the type of equity that you and I enjoy— things like upwardly mobile jobs with living wages, transportation, access to health care, and stable homes to live in. Furthermore, these beliefs that still influence our "free" society also exist within the walls of the modern church.

In truth, the assumptions about White supremacy that existed within the leadership at this particular church are what eventually functioned as a catalyst for my firing. While working at the church, I began to act upon my passion for helping impoverished individuals in the inner city. I wanted to bring the love of God to those who were living as marginalized figures and experiencing severe financial hardship—those who would have never stepped foot into the suburban church in which I was working. So, on my own time, I launched a campaign in order to raise funds for and awareness of a project for people experiencing homelessness, which would eventually turn into Love Beyond Walls. Momentum began to build as people became interested in the work that I was undertaking in order to serve the community. Relatively quickly, the lead pastor at the church became interested in the project, and indicated that the church and my organization should partner together. I was willing to hear him out even though I had obvious reservations. I understood that, if this pastor truly wanted to collaborate in order to bring social change and equality to our shared community, then I should be willing to team up as well.

However, I quickly realized that this pastor and I had very different ideas about how to move forward with our collaboration. He wanted me to shift the focus from the urban center to the suburban area in which the church was located. Therefore, not only was I dealing with blatant racism from other pastors on staff, but he wanted me to turn over the thing that God had placed on my heart. He also wanted the church to assume responsibility and decision-making power for various things, like branding any materials that I'd made with the church logo instead. I voiced my objections to moving our focus from the urban areas to the suburbs—as well as my objections to having the church branding on the materials that I'd made—and, a few weeks later, I found myself without a job. Without any warning or discussion, the pastor had decided to fire me. First discrimination and now fired.

I had neither been negligent in my duties to the church nor lost focus. What I had dared to do was to stand up against another potential injustice. I had not blindly tolerated a leadership decision that I did not agree with—shifting focus away from the struggling neighbors living on the margins of society to the suburban area in which the church was located. And while I can't be certain of what was going on in this pastor's heart, I can tell you that healthy collaboration always involves humility.

The ability to provide effective service in our communities depends greatly upon our capacity to collaborate well and put ourselves aside. It also depends on us regularly checking our motives. If we're not careful, sometimes what begins as wanting to make a positive impact on our society can slowly turn into wanting to receive accolades and praise.

When delivering a sermon to Ebenezer Baptist Church in 1968, Reverend Dr. Martin Luther King Jr. called our instinct to be seen "the Drum Major Instinct." He explained how this drive within us can lead us to dangerous places like exclusivism, superiority, racism, and even criminal acts. Yet he encouraged would-be leaders in how to properly steward the instinct, by paraphrasing the words of Jesus to his apostles:

> It's a good instinct if you use it right. It's a good instinct if you don't distort it and pervert it. Don't give it up. Keep feeling the need for being important. Keep feeling the need for being first. But I want you to be first in love. I want you to be first in moral excellence. I want you to be first in generosity. That is what I want you to do.[4]

First in love, moral excellence, and generosity: this is the life of a true servant and the only way to work effectively in collaboration for justice. This is how we take a stand together. We must take King's words to head and heart. He continued:

Yes, if you want to say that I was a drum major, say that I was a drum major for justice. Say that I was a drum major for peace. I was a drum major for right-eousness. And all of the other shallow things will not matter. I won't have any money to leave behind. I won't have the fine and luxurious things of life to leave behind. But I just want to leave a committed life behind. And that's all I want to say.

If I can help somebody as I pass along,
If I can cheer somebody with a word or song,
If I can show somebody he's traveling wrong,
Then my living will not be in vain.
If I can do my duty as a Christian ought,
If I can bring salvation to a world once wrought,
If I can spread the message as the master taught,
Then my living will not be in vain.[5]

If we truly want to make a difference, this is the stance that we must take: one of consistently running our mo-tives through this grid of selflessness and having the courage to leave our egos at the door.

IT TAKES FUSION

Of course, not all churches are like the one that I just de-scribed. I have had many positive experiences with churches who truly desire to influence their communities for the benefit of the greater good. One example is a meeting that I had with some church-planting mentors of mine, Brian and Amy. My wife and I were in the thick of things, trying to get a new kind of church off the ground: one that would be focused on outreach, on helping those on the margins. We were finding the process to be an extremely difficult one—so difficult, in fact, that we were ready to give up on our venture.

I remember feeling reluctant about telling our mentors this when we met with them over lunch one afternoon. I thought that they'd be disappointed in us. They had successfully planted hundreds of churches, yet there we were, ready to throw in the towel. When I finally found the courage to tell them how I was feeling, I couldn't believe Brian's response. He simply asked: "How has God shown up in your life?"

I hadn't been prepared for his question, but it immediately made me think of all that we'd been able to achieve through our organization, Love Beyond Walls. My wife and I had been able to collaborate with people from all walks of life—whether they were followers of Jesus or people who would never step foot in a church—in an effort to serve the most vulnerable. We'd been able to bring people in the community together to face the problems of impoverishment and homelessness.

When I started speaking about all of the amazing things that I'd witnessed, Brian interrupted to ask a few more pointed questions: "What if God wants you to do that? What if he's leading you to do that—what if that was your call?"

My wife, Cecilia, remembers vividly what it was like to go from an experience with leaders who had not cared to ask for our input to the supportive partnering of Brian and Amy. She says,

> Sometimes leaders don't think of the whole family and how church [conflict] situations can make you vulnerable because your kids are in children's ministry and, of course, have no idea what's happening. Having to pull them out because of a transition that wasn't even a real transition . . . It wasn't like, "Okay, let's see if you can continue Love Beyond Walls and make another location in the suburbs . . ." Our input was not asked. It was more, "This is what you are going to do and either you're on board or you're not." But Brian and Amy were interested in helping us figure out what was working with Love Beyond Walls and how they could help.

Brian and Amy, who wanted to partner with us, could have allowed ego and their desire to further their own status to take over, but they did anything but that. Instead, that afternoon, they helped to lead us toward what God was already doing in our lives and in the community at large. In just a few hours, they had walked us through the prerequisite steps to become an incorporated nonprofit organization and they became our very first donors!

They had the ability to be effective collaborators because they were able to identify how we were uniquely wired and encourage us to that end—not in order to make themselves look good but in order to make the largest possible impact for the common good. My mentors saw a dynamic leader in me who thrived on being "on the go" and righting the wrongs of injustices. They also knew that those aspects of my personality would flourish and benefit others most profoundly outside the walls of a church where I would not be limited by inflexible leadership or by logistics.

Eight years later, Brian and Amy are still partnering with our organization. Their initial support has helped make it possible for us to get people off the street, lead them to faith, reunite them with families, assist them in finding employment, and see them break addictions and recover the broken pieces of their lives. We've been able to donate over $2 million to the fights against poverty and homelessness and have even launched the nation's first museum for homelessness. We've had millions of in-kind items donated to our center to assist individuals who needed a helping hand during a tough time in their lives. All of this has been achieved, and has grown, from a little building in College Park.

COLLABORATING FOR SOCIAL CHANGE

There are people who are getting things done in the name of justice all over the world and standing together instead of allowing pride to hinder the work. Today there are organizations that are making sure that people in developing nations have access to clean drinking water. There are organizations that are rescuing young women and boys from sex trafficking. Some of these organizations are faith-based, while many are not. What they have in common is that they believe humans are worthy of dignity. The mission is to undertake the work of compassion, regardless of ideology.

These organizations are also fusing their efforts with other industries in order to bring about needed change for the economically disadvantaged. A prime example of this sort of collaboration is what Jasmine Crowe is doing at her organization, Goodr.[6] Jasmine launched her sustainable food waste technology company in Atlanta in 2017. Moved by the problem of hunger that she saw when she relocated to the city, Jasmine decided to do something about it.

What started out as a pop-up restaurant for the homeless in 2013 called "Sunday Soul" evolved into an app that acts as a liaison between the food-service industry and organizations that help lower-income people find their next meal. Goodr delivers leftover food from restaurants to meal-providing organizations like nonprofits, churches, and shelters. Through innovative thinking and collaboration, Jasmine is working not only to solve the problem of hunger but also to address the climate crisis, which is being worsened by the methane gas that is produced by the seventy-two billion pounds of food that are wasted in this country each year.[7]

Successful organizations like Goodr depend upon the collaboration of talented people who have not let isolation or the pursuit of financial security drive their actions. Instead, they have been driven by the desire to effect life-changing social impact.

Jay Bailey's work in helping to foster a spirit of entrepreneurship among the African American community in Atlanta, Georgia, is equally as interesting and important. Jay was named president and CEO of the Russell Center for Innovation and Entrepreneurship (RCIE) in 2018 after helping to raise leaders from underserved communities for over a decade. While serving as a leader in the nonprofit sector, he has made it his mission to increase financial literacy to empower communities to attain financial freedom. The RCIE building provides a place for entrepreneurs and innovators to create, to invent, "and learn while being engaged and motivated to develop game-changing new ideas to promote economic empowerment. . . . The center will [act] as a collaborative, co-working ecosystem that connects entrepreneurs to a customized curriculum, corporate partners, and access to capital."[8]

The RCIE will undoubtedly alter the social justice landscape, as people who would not previously have had access to this kind of resource begin both to hope for and attain a better quality of life. Through the RCIE, Jay is providing not just the material, technological, or employment resources that are needed to propel entrepreneurs forward in their careers but also life-changing empowerment toward financial growth. What Jay offers will undoubtedly benefit the community for several decades as those who benefit from his services invest back into the community, providing jobs, professional connections, and increased revenue.

FIND YOUR FIT

If we believe the false notion that our only opportunity to make a difference is to be found in the workplace— whether it be in a coffee shop or helping someone to their seat in a restaurant—we're missing out on a world that is so much bigger. You can serve in your community in a variety of ways. Get involved in ministry, join a nonprofit organization, and serve alongside people who are passionate about the same things that you are passionate about. You can become a foster parent. You can help find housing or jobs for people who are experiencing hardships. The list of ways in which you can contribute to the larger tapestry of community service is endless. Perhaps the easiest way in which to start is to begin by asking yourself questions like: "What do I wish would have been done for me when I was younger?" or "What kinds of stories make me respond with an increased level of emotion? How might I step into that space?"

When people ask themselves questions like these, they begin to see the needs of those around them so much more clearly. It's when we can see those needs, match them up with our personal skill set, and become proximate to those in need that a mission is born.

Cierra "Fly" Bobo followed this exact pattern. It was while working as a classroom teacher that she saw the need for more than just academic support for the young women she taught. She saw the significant gaps that were present in their life skills.[9] Bobo was able to identify their needs because of her own personal experience, growing up and searching for her own identity on the streets.

In order to combat the injustices found in schools that are located in low-income communities where young ladies often lack appropriate role models, she chose to partner with educators and start an afterschool mentoring program called FLY Life. The nonprofit organization's mission is to mentor and empower young women in the African American community to reach their highest potential:

> We will empower them to write a business plan, incorporate their businesses, develop a financial budget, open bank accounts, and create an opportunity for them to operate their business during the school year. Ultimately, we want to partner with major corporations and get them to offer our students their initial start-up funding and/or a scholarship to further their education.[10]

Impoverished communities across the nation need someone to see their need and decide to act. We can all do this. We all have something to contribute. Whether it's based on our skill set or our own past hurts, when we take the time to notice, we will see people who are struggling in ways that we might've struggled as well—or in ways in which we ourselves may have never struggled but with which we can nonetheless identify due to our common spiritual poverty.

It is this type of compassion for humanity that the Poor People's Campaign is calling for across the nation. It is a campaign that, having once been launched by the Reverend Dr. Martin Luther King Jr.,[11] has now been revived by the Reverend Dr. William Barber II, and is a call for nationwide "moral revival." The campaign, called Moral Mondays, rallies people from all walks of life to stand up for human rights like health care for all and protests against voter suppression. What first began in North Carolina has become a larger movement, and regardless of religious affiliation, the attendees at these events share a common belief that our country must do better for the oppressed and marginalized. Protesters engage in civil disobedience for the common good. One of the organization's founding principles states:

> Whereas the distorted moral narrative of religious nationalism blames poor and oppressed people for our poverty and oppression, our deepest religious and constitutional values insist that the primary moral issues of our day must be how our society treats the poor, those on the margins, women, LGBTQIA2S+ folks, workers, immigrants, the disabled and the sick; equal protection under the law; and the desire for peace, love and harmony within and among nations.[12]

Moral Mondays are an example of people coming together for the common good as opposed to fighting solely for their individual rights. Regardless of which side of the aisle we sit on, when we see people going hungry or left without basic health services, we can all agree that we wouldn't want that for our own families. What will we do as humans to stand up for other humans?

This is the noblest and highest calling: to do what is necessary to ensure that every human being has access to what they need to care for themselves and their families. Every human should be allowed the chance to succeed. I want to challenge you to begin to think through the issues that face your own community. The truth is that this mission requires each and every one of us to stand up for those who cannot stand up for themselves.

Who are the people who are on the front lines in your community? Where are the gaps in services for the underserved people in your community or neighboring communities? What specific skill set do you bring to the table? Maybe the answer is that you don't know what your unique skills are—and that's okay. Often the best way to uncover our particular makeup of skills and talents is within the community that we find ourselves drawn to.

CHAPTER SIX

KNOW YOUR WORTH AND MAKE A DIFFERENCE

For some of us, as we've seen, feelings of superiority can keep us from noticing and helping meet the needs of others. For others of us, one of the that things that prevents us from undertaking activities that would aid the pursuit of justice is the false idea that we have nothing to offer someone who is suffering, and nothing of value to lend to a complex justice issue. We incorrectly believe that we are unable to make a difference because we lack financial means, expertise, or influence. This is one of the most dangerous lies that there is. Often it is the biggest hurdle we face on the path to finding our own social justice fight. The truth is that the world needs each and every one of us. Every major movement toward social equality was able to gain traction because of the hands, skills, resources, and thoughts of many individuals, regardless of their particular financial means or status.

The Montgomery Bus Boycott—a pivotal moment in the history of the civil rights movement—is a profound example of what can happen when people realize that they can, indeed, meaningfully contribute to a cause by sharing their own resources, no matter how small or limited those resources might be. You're probably familiar with the story of Rosa Parks, an African American activist who, in 1955, was arrested for refusing to vacate her seat for a White bus patron. Though Rosa had already been undertaking justice work with her husband for many years prior to this famous incident, to this day she is most remembered for the extraordinary level of personal courage that she displayed in choosing to stand her ground. It was her courage that would galvanize an oppressed group of people into action. The Montgomery Bus Boycott was able to sustain itself for a whole year afterward, thanks to the solidarity of a group of people who came together to offer whatever they had. One educational history website summarizes the movement in this way:

> Although African Americans represented at least 75 percent of Montgomery's bus ridership, the city resisted complying with the protester's demands. To ensure the boycott could be sustained, black leaders organized carpools, and the city's African American taxi drivers charged only 10 cents—the same price as bus fare—for African American riders. Many black residents chose simply to walk to work or other destinations. Black leaders organized regular mass meetings to keep African American residents mobilized around the boycott.[1]

What's being described here is a vast social network that was created by a people who were weary of being mistreated and were ready to take action. Each person who was involved in this collective effort to battle injustice gave what they were able to give in terms of their own resources—whether it was a ride to work or a word of encouragement from the pulpit to motivate and inspire others to continue the fight.[2] I'm sure that many of them even battled the same thoughts we do now, such as *What can I offer?* Sometimes, as in the case of the Black taxi drivers who charged passengers less for their fares in the context of the boycott, what they had to offer was a personal sacrifice—one that they had committed to make for the sake of the greater good.

The pursuit of social justice in today's world is no different. Our collective effort to change this world for the better requires us to stand up to fear as well as cultivate and harness our ability to work together to bring about change, offering what we have for the sake of others. Every single contribution matters when we are taking a stand together. Rosa Parks offered her courage to her community; her community, in turn, offered physical resources like cars as well as abstract resources like time, as people chose to walk to their various destinations instead of taking the bus, thereby snubbing public transportation in solidarity with Rosa Parks and the civil rights movement. Everyone had something to offer. You do too.

A LITTLE GOES A LONG WAY

Understanding that we have something to offer can be difficult if we believe that we must already have figured everything out about a specific issue or that we must be able to provide an expert level of advice if we are to become involved with a particular cause or campaign. Or, if we're busy people—like most of us are—we might be under the false impression that we have to devote an excessive or unreasonable amount of time to a project in order to be of real use or value. The truth is that by showing even just a few hours of dedication to an individual or an organization, we can make a substantial and lasting positive impact.

MENTOR: The National Mentoring Partnership is a nonprofit agency dedicated to pairing over nine million children who would otherwise be facing life without a significant adult role model to whom they can turn with a healthy, caring adult mentor. The agency's work has shown that, when students have a stable adult mentor, their lives are unquestionably improved in almost every way. Everything from the rate of a young person's academic progress to the likelihood of their future economic stability is increased when a mentor enters their life. Such individuals are even 130 percent more likely to hold leadership positions in the future as a result of their mentoring relationships.[3]

Imagine offering just a few hours of your time each month to provide a listening ear to a young person who is in the midst of all the angst and worry that can accompany adolescence. You wouldn't believe how monumental your presence could feel to someone who has never been able to experience uninterrupted time with a trusted adult whose sole purpose is to help them to get through life and to offer compassion. Doing so does not require that you have an advanced degree or an abundance of either time or money. It simply requires attention. What that young person needs is for you to be there for them.

Perhaps you're passionate about sports. Imagine using that passion to spend some time on a basketball court with a young person who shares your interest and has no one else with whom they can enjoy one-to-one time in such a way. Or maybe the motivation to get involved is rooted a little bit deeper than that for you. Maybe you understand what it's like to grow up without having a significant adult figure in your life and, as such, want to be able to do something meaningful that helps a young person navigate their way through such hurt. There are always a number of issues to which we can give our time or finances or expertise. But it's typically at the intersection of own past hurts and current passions where we find our true cause to champion: the issue by which we're most profoundly moved and for which we can make the biggest impact in the lives of others.

That is exactly what happened for my friend Jamil. In 2014, when Jamil came to volunteer with us, Love Beyond Walls was starting a mobile makeover unit in order to provide clothing, a barber shop, and a hygiene station for the underserved community. This twenty-seven-year-old man was so excited to volunteer that I remember being blown away. He was attending a nearby barbering school at the time and offered his services as a barber. I hadn't expected a young man like Jamil, busy building his career, to want to give so many hours to volunteering. But I soon found out that Jamil had personal reasons for becoming more proximate to his community. He confessed to me that he hadn't seen his father since his high school graduation and that he knew that his father was living on the streets. His hope was to one day encounter his father on our makeover bus.

It took an extreme level of vulnerability for Jamil to place himself on that bus every day. But he did so precisely because he found himself at the intersection of a personal passion for the cause and his own skill set. And although he wanted to see his father, there would, of course, be obvious emotional hills to climb as a result of doing so. What if after seeing his father once, the relationship did not continue? What if his father turned out to be in really bad shape? What if old wounds were reopened? Jamil allowed himself to be vulnerable in spite of all the questions, and after just one month of volunteering, he did indeed have the chance to see his father.

I remember being on Martin Luther King Jr. Boulevard when Jamil's father climbed aboard our bus. He hadn't known that his son had become a barber or, indeed, anything about what had transpired in Jamil's life over the past ten years. Seeing them reconnect made me feel so happy for the two of them. I watched as they embraced one another after Jamil's father had received a haircut. They decided to stay in contact, and after a few weeks, I asked Jamil how his dad was doing. Amazingly, his father had enrolled in a drug rehabilitation program and found a job— and his own apartment too! He'd also reunited with Jamil's brother. Jamil believes his experience on that bus with his father and with the other members of the homeless community was powerful—not just for the community members but for himself as well. "It was therapeutic in a way," he says, "hearing people's stories and sharing stories. And all of that just through a haircut."

But it wasn't just a haircut that Jamil gave his father or any of the other people who boarded our bus. The changes that occurred in his father's life were due to the profound power of being seen by someone. That moment of reconnection with Jamil—and the subsequent talks that he held with both Jamil and his brother—left him feeling worthy again. His dignity was being restored, moment by moment, all because Jamil had decided to use his skills intentionally as a barber in order to serve. And this intentionality led to a renewed relationship with his father.

OFFER YOUR HANDS AND FEET

Jesus lived his life this way, intentionally prioritizing ministry. He often stopped in the middle of a journey with his disciples to tend to the needs of an individual, allowing himself to be interrupted by God's work. Even on his way over to Jairus's house to bring his daughter back to life,

Jesus stopped to heal a woman who had a chronic medical condition (see Matthew 9:18-26). This is the kind of work to which God calls us; make time for such work while en route to your own destinations.

Or we might even be fortunate enough to be able to make time within activities we're already a part of.

I think of my friends Aaron and Michelle, who lead a small congregation in Austin, Texas. The community of people who make up their church are not affluent; they are a people of lower incomes who have made the commitment to serve others anyway. Some of the congregants either fall below the poverty line or are homeless themselves.

When Aaron and Michelle contacted our organization about partnering in our Love Sinks In campaign, it was with the intention of caring for their local homeless population during the Covid-19 pandemic. Per the United States government and the CDC's recommendation of best practices for Covid-19 prevention, handwashing was at the top of the list. However, individuals experiencing homelessness do not have access to soap and water. We launched Love Sinks In as a direct response to that reality. As the rest of the world was talking about sanitizing, fighting over toilet tissue, and complaining about staying inside, Love Beyond Walls was thinking about an entire community of homeless people—over half a million people—who would have given anything to have a safe, warm place to lay their heads. Our immediate goal with the Love Sinks In campaign was to install as many portable wash stations as possible based on collaboration with local stakeholders, governors, mayors, private sectors, and philanthropic partners across America. What Aaron and Michelle found is that their partnership with the campaign has also served their congregants in some unforeseen ways.

The church's small groups each "adopted" a sink, meaning that the group members rotate who goes out to service the sink each week by filling it back up with water and soap or cleaning it with disinfectant. However, in the middle of maintaining the sinks, they've been able to cultivate relationships with those struggling with homelessness, and dismantle some stereotypes along the way. Because of these relationships, they no longer believe that all homeless people are lazy or drug addicts or simply panhandling and then going home to a nice house. Michelle explains,

> What's been encouraging is that the members of our church have slowed down and taken time to actually talk with the people around the sink and begin building relationships with people. As is often the case, there are immediate needs like socks, T-shirts, toothpaste, and all of a sudden there is a relationship being built with people from our church. They are hearing their [the homeless community's] stories, dispelling some of the myths that people have about them.

Real relationships are forming in small increments of time, by small group members in a church giving just a bit of themselves—together. It reminds me of the early church in the book of Acts—how God moved in their community, and how they were deeply committed to each other and felt a responsibility toward one another. And how they had all things in common (Acts 2:43-47).

OPPORTUNITIES TO BRING JUSTICE ARE EVERYWHERE

Whether you start by serving multiple times per week like Jamil or join a rotating monthly serving schedule like the congregants at Aaron and Michelle's church, the opportunities for bringing justice and restoration are everywhere. You might also decide to join an organization that is doing things on the other side of the globe.

I'm inspired by people like Carlos Rodriguez, for example. Carlos is an author, a preacher, and the founder and CEO of the Happy NPO.[4] His nonprofit organization works to bring social and economic relief to those who need it the most. Focusing on the "poorest of the poor," Carlos and his team are on the ground in places like Puerto Rico, where disaster relief continues after hurricanes and earthquakes have left people without the basic necessities of life like water, electricity, and food.[5] Though many people come to help in the weeks that immediately follow a natural disaster, only a select few will stay beyond the news cycle of the story. Carlos is one who has stayed. One of his campaigns is called the Blue Roof Fund, named for the hundreds of blue tarpaulins that are currently acting as makeshift roofs for Puerto Rico's citizens. In partnership with local nonprofit agencies, Carlos's goal is to help to restore homes and businesses there. The Happy NPO offers to host anyone who has an interest in serving; individuals can stay with them while engaging in such work.[6]

There are also justice activists like my friend Shaun King. As a writer, podcaster, and cofounder of Real Justice PAC, Shaun and his team are fighting for political reform within our justice system by employing new political strategies—ones that rally voters behind one major issue. Currently, he is mobilizing a new generation of voters to elect officials such as district attorneys who will fight the policies that are endemic in structural racism.[7]

Shaun uses social media to inform and inspire as well as to right the wrongs of our justice system. He was instrumental in the 2019 internet campaign to save Rodney Reed, a fifty-one-year-old man from Texas who was due to be executed for a crime, even though substantial evidence had suggested he was innocent. The petition to stay the execution of this man succeeded, having attained nearly three million signatures; it was the fastest-growing human rights petition of all time.[8] It has provided Rodney with an opportunity to regain his freedom if the courts exonerate him.[9] Shaun continues to use his social media platform to rally his followers to commit small but impactful acts for justice.

Both Carlos and Shaun are engaged in serving humanity by righting wrongs, but their fights are different. As is mine and as will yours be. And that's okay. In fact, it's more than okay. The world needs you to be you, so that you might influence your particular sphere. It might mean that your fight looks quieter.

As you move toward a meaningful life of working for social justice, you might be wondering what you ought to do first. You're ready to move forward and create a purposeful lifestyle of serving, but perhaps you're still unsure of your own areas of passion. If that's the case, I challenge you to start asking yourself some tough questions about your own history with justice. What have some of your own past hurts looked like? And, at this very moment, what issues keep coming up that you feel strongly about? It is responding to these questions—along with learning to ponder the problems that your community faces—that will help you begin to find your unique calling.

GET EDUCATED

Every community has a different set of challenges, and unpacking exactly which issues face yours is paramount to learning where you're needed. So begin to ask questions. Look around at your own community. What do you see?

The question may sound trite, but we all know how self-absorbed our lifestyles can become. Our days are full of routine and tunnel vision. We arrive at our job or at our child's school in auto-pilot mode, missing everything from the new restaurant that's opened a few blocks down the road to the homeless woman who sits on the bench that's just outside the mini-mart, next to our gym.

I encourage you to begin taking notice, whether it's through slowing down and opening your eyes, listening more intentionally in conversations with neighbors, or joining a community message board online. The needs of your community will begin to make themselves known.

A more overt method of understanding the struggles of your particular community might be to attend a city council meeting. Although the majority of these meetings are public, the percentage of citizens who attend them is extremely low. A survey taken in over two hundred communities between the years of 2012 and 2014 found that 81 percent of people had never contacted a local elected official, and 76 percent had never attended a public meeting.[10] Even if your desire is not to be involved in politics, letting your voice be heard in a meeting in which key decisions are being made would be a step in the right direction, especially in advocating for the rights and resources of people who may not be able to stand up for themselves. For example, a single mother who is working two jobs in order to support her family is unlikely to have the time to attend a public meeting. However, you might be able to step in as her voice, asking for better afterschool programs or higher-quality lunches to be provided in public schools. Similarly, you might become the voice of a veteran experiencing homelessness, advocating for more housing and free citywide resources for those who have served their country. The ways in which we can stand—both literally and figuratively—arm-in-arm with those who are suffering are limitless.

We can advocate for others, knowing that our time is a valuable resource.

We can also become more educated about the larger, more systemic problems that underlie justice issues. For example, you may begin to wonder about the fact that, although your community seems racially diverse, there also seems to be a dividing line when it comes to who inhabits the apartments and rental homes in the community versus who is able to own a home just a street or two away. Is the economic disparity between people of color and their White counterparts what you're seeing play out?

A 2018 article by the Center for American Progress explains how a history of discrimination and structural racism has led to the continuing disparity in wealth between Black and White people, even as educational opportunities have increased. For example, here are just a few of the policies the authors cite as key to the economic gap:

A well-documented history of mortgage market discrimination means that blacks are significantly less likely to be homeowners than whites, which means they have less access to the savings and tax benefits that come with owning a home. Persistent labor market discrimination and segregation also force blacks into fewer and less advantageous employment opportunities than their white counterparts. Thus, African Americans have less access to stable jobs, good wages, and retirement benefits at work—all key drivers by which American families gain access to savings.[11]

Systemic policies like these serve to keep an entire group of people from progressing economically and are what often undergird the problems that we see in our communities. But when these policies do not negatively affect our own lives, they can be easy to ignore. The quest for equal justice for all requires us not to ignore these types of policies or cracks in the system but to educate ourselves about them and then become agents of change.

Social justice work requires us to dig a little deeper for answers—and those answers are rarely simple. This is why we are all required to participate in the fight. Each of us will come to a scenario with different experiences, passions, expertise, and ideas for better solutions.

CHAPTER SEVEN

TAKE THE FIRST STEP

My friend Mike Fye started volunteering regularly with Love Beyond Walls because he had experienced extreme levels of poverty himself and was moved by the people he met through the organization. Though he was a young single man—in his twenties—he quickly became a staple among our families, doing whatever he could and listening keenly so as to identify further opportunities to serve. He knew families by name and helped to provide services like offering rides to work or spending time with children whose parents perhaps needed a break. He offered whatever he could and whatever he knew. It was Mike's openness that led to his forming a special bond with one of our community members, Kenan, whom Mike now refers to as his "brother."

One Wednesday, Mike had spotted Kenan passing by our Love Feeds program. Kenan was about the same age as Mike. When he rode past our building on a rickety-looking bike, he was half-dressed and obviously in need of help. He didn't stop for help, though. Mike went after him, asking if he could be of some assistance, but Kenan was stand-offish, saying that he didn't need anything. It was clear that he was having a rough time, but Mike didn't want to push too hard, especially given that it was the first time they'd ever met. There was something about Kenan that Mike strongly identified with though, even though he had spoken with him only briefly. Mike himself remembered struggling to ask for help when he'd needed it the most. So, although Kenan left that day without saying much and without accepting any resources, Mike remained persistent and consistent in his approach and was ready to help when Kenan returned the following week. Over time, Kenan began to open up about the various things with which he was struggling. Eventually, Mike was even able to make the necessary arrangements for Kenan to obtain a new bike.

Mike and Kenan found that they were not all that different from one another. Yes, they were living in different circumstances, but their lives were not dissimilar in the ways that truly matter. They had both experienced poverty to some extent while they were growing up; exchanging their stories helped them form a connection—a bond—that opened the door to having a real relationship. Mike and Kenan found community with one another, and Mike eventually encouraged him to go back to school.

The initial reason Mike had been attracted to our organization was because of his past challenges, but he quickly found community and became a leader as well as one of our most committed volunteers. He pushed past any fear that he had, taking that first step to see how he could be of help. Gradually, the small contributions that he offered to our community in terms of his time and resources amounted to something very significant. He made people feel seen. He helped many of them reestablish their dignity when they had felt unworthy of receiving support and care. When people from our community see him, they know that it's genuine and not manufactured.

It's truly what being together means. Mike's ability to show up every single week, hold conversations, and stop by to check on our community members made the community feel like he was more than a volunteer. They started to see him as family. His care, attention to details, and respect for our community screamed of authenticity. Of course, Mike is not perfect but showing up with his presence made the love of God shine forth through him perfectly.

FIND YOUR INSPIRATION

Unsurprisingly, many people who undertake social justice work have been affected personally by the issue they get involved in. It is incredibly powerful to see someone who has come out on the other side of addiction step into the role of a counselor or an advocate for someone else who is currently facing the very same struggle. Equally, it is immeasurably moving to watch a single mother—who remembers the struggle of raising children alone—step in to be a source of encouragement and support for other young women who are in the same scenario. However, in a world that is full of problems of injustice, there is no correct way in which to identify the particular issue with which you should become involved. Your fight may be found in what makes you burn with frustration or what lights you up with joy.

Yet even with a desire to help firmly in place, it's natural to feel a bit nervous about the process of becoming involved in justice projects. My hope is to empower you to move beyond your fear.

My friend Maria has been qualified as a physician in the United Kingdom for four years and has been training as an eye surgeon, but she has felt strongly called to do something for God beyond her professional work. However, sometimes people in highly skilled careers struggle to clearly see how their proficiencies translate into other areas. They can even disqualify themselves from important work before getting started, out of fear of not being an expert in that field the way they are in their own careers. These were points of worry for Maria that initially held her back from leaning into the service she had a calling for.

During the coronavirus pandemic, she was redeployed to work on the high-dependency Covid-19 wards at her hospital, turning her professional world upside down. In this new environment, she had to adapt her skills as an eye surgeon in order to overcome the extreme challenges she was facing in fighting the virus for her patients. During this work, she became acutely aware of the barriers to health care people of color continue to face. The mortality rate of

Covid-19 is significantly higher for people of color,[1] but they have also been battling racial disparities within modern-day health care systems for much longer. In the United Kingdom, Black women are five times more likely to die during pregnancy and after childbirth compared to White women. For women of mixed ethnicity, the risk is three times greater, and for Asian women, it is twice as high.[2] The figures are equally shocking in the United States.[3] These realities led Maria to delve further into issues of racial injustice and fired up her passion for the subject.

As a physician, she had developed organizational skills, attention to detail, a strong work ethic, and people management skills that she decided to put to use in her own church community. As an indigenous Egyptian, she recognized how her own community wrestled with their identity and saw this as an opportunity to strengthen the church's response to racial injustices. She wanted to educate people and create a space for them to come together to learn about these topics. So she put together a team and organized an online conference to provide spiritual and educational talks on the many facets of racism within society's infrastructure. Her team researched, prepared material, identified speakers, advertised, and promoted on online platforms.

Our discussions early on during this process encouraged her to identify the potential for service that lay within her existing skills, without her needing to immediately be an expert on the issues she was passionate about. And the success of this conference broke racial, generational, and geographic barriers—during a pandemic! People from across the country attended to learn more. The conference afforded them the opportunity to develop deeper understanding of and empathy for others, and they left with opened hearts, changed perceptions, and a hunger to learn more about their marginalized brothers and sisters.

The Bible offers countless examples of how God calls those who may not feel that they have been gifted with any specific expertise or talent but who have, nonetheless, been blessed with a special understanding of the lived experience of struggle that empowers them to lead others to a better way of life. Think, for example, of Moses, whom God used as an instrument to free the Israelites from bondage and to bring them to a place of restoration, even though he described himself as being "slow of speech and slow of tongue" (Exodus 4:10). His compassion for the plight of his people and his frustration toward their oppressor made Moses the ideal candidate for the task, regardless of his shortcomings as a communicator. God often calls on us to help draw others out of dark and painful places specifically because of our ability to understand such pain on a deep level.

For my wife and I, Love Beyond Walls was an organic outcome of the ways in which both of our lives had been affected by poverty. Nonetheless, we still had to fight through feelings of inadequacy, and we struggled in the beginning. Gaining traction in order to launch successful campaigns was difficult, especially as social media was not yet popular at the time. We had been doing the work of engaging the homeless community for almost fifteen years before anyone knew who we were. Working out of a garage, we attempted to raise awareness of our organization and our work and sent text messages to everyone we knew, trying to rally volunteers for a service event. But text message services were rather basic then too, so it was not possible to send group texts in the way that you can now. You can imagine just how time-consuming individually texting people proved to be. And sometimes, of course, people would tell my wife or myself that they were going to show up to volunteer at one of our events—only to fail to show up in the end. It was a discouraging time for us to say the least. I desperately wanted people to support some of the unconventional campaigns that we'd launched later when Love Beyond Walls was a formal organization—like the mobile makeover unit, for example—but nothing seemed to be working out in the way that we'd planned. We felt like barrier after barrier were being placed in front of our mission and its progress. Our inability to reach a larger audience—coupled with the challenge of finding volunteers—caused us to fear that we wouldn't be able to succeed.

It wasn't until we came up with a seemingly radical idea on Thanksgiving of 2014 that the momentum changed. On that day, I decided to live on top of the bus for thirty days. Given that I am an introvert, it might seem odd that I would do something that would get as much attention as living on a bus, but big, dramatic ideas are often what God has used in my life to produce successful campaigns. Once I even raised awareness for homelessness by walking over seven hundred miles in a March Against Poverty campaign and over four hundred miles in a follow-up campaign to that one called MAP18.

A church in Georgia donated a bus to us and we needed to bring attention to our cause and use awareness to mobilize groups of people to get involved to actually transform it. We were over at a friend's house at the time and as we were thinking about what I could do to bring attention to it, I casually said, "What should I do, live on top of the bus?" My wife responded, "That's it! That is what you will do." My wife encouraged me to live on top of a bus for an entire month to bring attention to the project and raise funds to help transform it. Our friends Dave and Jen whose house we were over at when the idea came about agreed to help out. Dave had carpentry skills and agreed to lead any volunteers and help transform the bus afterward. When I first got on top on the bus on a safe platform that Dave built, I felt embarrassed. The sheer nature of doing something public creates a lot of vulnerability. Would people listen to me? Would people respond? Would they get involved? All those questions and more I wrestled with. But the biggest lesson that my wife and I learned during this process is that God provides for what honors God. As we advocated, God sent both the people and resources to transform this bus into Atlanta's first makeover bus. The same bus that Jamil met his father on.

If the idea of living on a bus for thirty days or walking hundreds of miles makes you nervous, that's okay. In fact, that's wonderful. It means you're just wired differently than I am. Each of us approaching justice work in different ways is vitally important to covering every facet of the battle to restore dignity. There are many movements that have started quietly but made a huge impact. Some have even started behind phones or computer screens. I believe that we all have unique skillsets that we readily use in places that feel very comfortable to us, but if we are thinking about having greater impact, you must be willing to take the step and risk using your skills in areas that may feel unnatural at first. We must be willing to follow the Lord's lead step by step in the fight against injustice, even if you can't see the big picture, or if you don't know if you'll succeed or feel afraid. It is during these moments we must allow the compassion of the issue that is close to our hearts push us toward making the step and taking the risk. Doing what comes naturally to us is important in finding our particular purpose in serving.

TAKE ACTION THAT FEELS NATURAL

The hashtag #MeToo gained popularity amidst allegations of sexual abuse by dozens of female celebrities against Harvey Weinstein in 2017, which later resulted in his incarceration. But Me Too movement founder, Tarana Burke, always envisioned more for the movement than simply one abuser at a time going to jail. Her focus was on taking a hard look at the systems that allow sexual abuse to continue. In a 2020 interview with the *Harvard Gazette*, Tarana said:

> What I think, and I hope, is that we're in a place that's moving away from the individual headlines and salacious stories about accusations being made toward individuals, and thinking more collectively about what we can do to end sexual violence and how we are shifting the focus away from individual bad acts and moving it toward the systemic cause of sexual violence.[4]

In one year, the hashtag was used nineteen million times on Twitter and still continues to produce movement in the pursuit of justice for victims of sexual abuse. People stood together to lend their voice to a human rights issue in a way that felt natural to them, via their phones or computers. It's a reminder that actions can be taken right from where we are.[5]

For example, in 2019 the congregation of Christian Assembly Church in Los Angeles partnered with the nonprofit organization RIP Medical Debt in order to eliminate $5.3 million in medical debt as a Christmas gift to their community.[6] The church decided to surprise those families in their congregation who earned less than twice the federal poverty line and were consequently having to deal with medical debt. Co-lead pastor Tom Hughes highlighted the generosity of the church community as well as the generosity of God as he explained why the church had made such a decision. "As they recover from their illness," he said of those who would benefit from the debt relief, "it'll help them get back on their feet, and avoid homelessness. All of this is being done in Jesus' name."[7]

People saw the needs within their own church body and decided to do something to serve their fellow congregants well. They gathered their own resources and partnered effectively in order to bring about a greater good. When we are moved to action that feels natural to our various communities and spheres of influence—be they inside or outside of the church—we form a powerful and dynamic network of change-makers.

Across the globe, Sarah Corbett decided to embrace what came naturally to her as an introverted person. Calling herself a "Craftivist," Sarah uses crafting to get a social justice message out into the world. In her TED Talk, she discusses a campaign she was involved in where she and other crafters designed beautiful, small scrolls of paper that contained messages about how clothing is produced. They then "shop-dropped" (instead of shoplifted) the scrolls into pockets of clothing being sold in stores using unethical practices. Sarah says she wants people to think about questions like, "What's the story behind your clothes? Is it a joyful story of how it's made, or is it a torturous one?"[8]

Each of us can play an integral part in our community, contributing various valuable resources such as the alleviation of financial burdens or solidarity for a movement. Our fight will not always be found in something we've suffered through ourselves. Sometimes, we find it by embracing a persistent sense of compassion toward a particular group, or we find that someone's story of struggle won't leave us as we close our eyes to go to sleep. In this case, paying attention to our emotional responses to the stories that we hear is key to discovering our fight. Whether it's a story that you watch on the nightly news, something you run across on your social media feed, or even a story that has been shared among your friendship group—pay special attention. The beginnings of your fight might be right in front of you.

PAY ATTENTION AND BECOME AN ALLY

When I decided to walk those four hundred miles from Atlanta to Memphis in 2018, there were times when I was scared. Especially as I walked through certain neighborhoods in which I knew intense prejudice existed. I even faced some of it myself. I was stopped by the police for ostensibly "disturbing the peace," as well as threatened by a driver who had a Confederate flag sticker. I'm not sure what would have happened to me had I been alone on the journey. Thankfully, I had a supportive group of people who were looking out for me, following me in a van to keep an eye on things to ensure that I was okay. Without having that support system, I probably would have given up on the venture at times when I just didn't know if what I was doing was going to make any difference at all—or at times when I even thought that my life was in danger.

Partners are everything when we stand up to an issue. Perhaps you wouldn't consider yourself a "justice worker" per se, but if you can walk alongside someone—literally or figuratively—who is doing hard work to bring about equality, then you are doing good and righteous work too. Those who fight consistently for justice on behalf of others will come up against challenges that stretch them to the breaking point. There have been times when I've been unsure of a campaign's prospects of success and have needed people to encourage me as well as to come in and fight alongside me. Some of the friends who have fought together with me have not even been directly connected to the issue at hand themselves. Not everyone who volunteers at Love Beyond Walls has a personal history with homelessness—but they all have a passion for restoring dignity to those who are suffering. This kind of social justice worker is no less powerful than the one who has experienced certain traumas; they can make just as big of an impact when they're willing to listen carefully to the stories of others and seek to identify with the spiritual poverty that is often found at the core of social injustices.

We're seeing this more and more in movements like Black Lives Matter (BLM), where non-Black allies have joined protests across the world in support of not just Black lives but what they see as a stand for human dignity. They are joining their Black brothers and sisters in efforts of solidarity. BLM cofounder Alicia Garza said in an interview, "I have friends texting me with their images in

France and the Netherlands and Costa Rica, and people are showing me that they are showing up in solidarity."[9]

Allies are indispensable to any fight for justice. I think of men who have been moved by the stories told by their female friends, daughters, wives, mothers, or girlfriends and who are standing up for the equal treatment of women by joining campaigns like the Women's March in 2017 and fighting for the elimination of long-tolerated sexual harassment. As women become more vocal about their history of harassment, men listening and taking action is imperative to the realization of justice. Initiatives like HeforShe, launched by UN Women in 2014, is empowering male supporters to engage in women's equality efforts within their communities.[10] Everyone from heads of state who have the power to enact policy change[11] to everyday fathers who are teaching their sons to stand up to the mistreatment of girls on the baseball field[12] is helping to usher in a new age of equality among the sexes.

We can look to Jesus and the example of his treatment of the adulterous woman in the book of John to see how God intervenes on behalf of women who are facing persecution. In the story, the woman caught committing adultery has been sentenced to be stoned. Looking at her accusers, Jesus challenges them by saying: "Let him who is without sin among you be the first to throw a stone at her" (John 8:7 ESV). Jesus does not shy away from the need and responsibility to stand up for those who are not heard by the leaders of their day or the dominant culture.

Although we may not personally be affected by the unfair treatment of women, men who stand with women understand something of vital importance: that social injustices must be fought by a community of people that comprises not only those who are directly impacted but also those who stand in solidarity with them. Men must be taught by other men to treat women equitably, holding each other to a standard of accountability that calls out certain behaviors as being unacceptable. Whether we're directly affected by a particular social injustice or not, the power of true change rests in the hands of a collective body, and your local community is a great place to begin.

FINDING YOUR PLACE AMONG OTHERS

Finding people to serve alongside and taking the time to identify the role that best suits you are of the highest importance. You can start by researching groups in your community who are already undertaking work to eradicate the social justice issue that you are most interested in.

Technology is an excellent tool when it comes to connecting with a social justice fight. You can run a basic internet search by entering in a particular issue and your zip code to see what you discover. You can also use specific social media hashtags to find nonprofit campaigns. You can even utilize helpful websites like VolunteerMatch, which connects volunteers to the cause that is right for them. Within minutes of creating a profile—based on your interests, skills, and geographical location—several nonprofit organizations in your area will be recommended to you.[13]

Purposity is another organization using technology to change the ways in which people interact with service opportunities within their communities. The organization's app acts as a liaison between nonprofit agencies and school districts, for example—groups that are knowledgeable about the needs of the community—and the everyday citizen who would like to do something to help their neighbor. The app sends notifications to the user's phone about the needs in their area. A user can then pay for a needed item for someone who is experiencing economic hardship and Purposity will deliver it.[14]

Once you've found an organization or group that is undertaking the work that best suits you, it's wise to consider other factors too. For example, you may arrive to serve in a shelter and realize that you much prefer connecting with the community through conversation over setting up tables or cleaning up. Or you may discover the reverse: that because you have a more introverted personality, work that is more "behind the scenes" would be preferable for you. In either case, both roles are vital to the operation of any organization. And although the first priority must be to serve wherever we are needed, if possible, it's best to serve in relation to our strengths. Speak with the volunteer coordinator of the organization and ask about the roles that are available. It's likely that they have more than enough needs to address, meaning that you can help out in another area if necessary.

Increasingly, employers are using personality assessments like Myers-Briggs, CliftonStrengths, 16 Personalities, or the Enneagram to place people in appropriate teams for their skill sets or to assess whether or not someone is a good fit for the role for which they are applying. Utilizing the same strategy to find your place within a volunteer organization could be valuable for you as you enter into a place where many different skills are needed.

PERSONALITY RESOURCE GUIDE

Myers-Briggs
www.myersbriggs.org/my-mbti-personality-type

CliftonStrengths
www.gallup.com/cliftonstrengths/en/253676/how-clifton strengths-works.aspx

16 Personalities
www.16personalities.com

Spiritual Gifts Survey
https://gifts.churchgrowth.org/spiritual-gifts-survey

Emotional Intelligence Quiz
www.ihhp.com/free-eq-quiz

The Road Back to You: An Enneagram Journey to Self-Discovery *by Ian Morgan Cron and Suzanne Stabile*
www.ivpress.com/the-road-back-to-you

Enneagram Institute
www.enneagraminstitute.com

The Synergist: How to Lead Your Team to Predictable Success *by Les McKeown*
https://us.macmillan.com/books/9780230120556

Aside from your personality type and how you are wired as an individual, you should also consider your resources when examining what role would suit you best. Everyone will not be out in front. Maybe you're a teacher who can educate his or her students by incorporating more awareness of social justice issues into your daily curriculum. Maybe you're a blogger who can use your platform to bring attention to those who are suffering and how your followers might be of service in their communities. It all counts. The only thing we need to all have in common is our shared determination and commitment to fight to address social justice issues. What you can bring to an organization is not limited to the skills that you'd bring to your vocation—it includes your hobbies and the things that bring a smile to your face. It even includes the people you know, and the people they know. No matter how you decide to serve, your intentionality in deciding to use your gifts and leveraging the gifts of others will matter a great deal when you take your step to take a stand.

CHAPTER EIGHT

LIVE INTENTIONALLY

All of us have an innate desire to ensure that by the time we leave this world, we have meant something to someone or made a difference somewhere. We want to know that our lives were not lived in vain, and that we had purpose and made an impact. When we see those whom we admire fighting for the good of others, mending broken systems, or creating organizations that help others thrive, we're inspired, and allow ourselves to dream big about the ways we might do similar things. However, most of us don't make the necessary space in our lives to actually accomplish the things about which we've been dreaming. Those who do make the space are those who are willing to live disrupted lives. They are those who are willing to disrupt their normal routines so that they might accomplish the work of God. I call them agents of disruption. In one of his most memorable tweets, John Lewis described an agent of disruption as someone who is "never afraid to make some noise and get in good trouble, necessary trouble."[1]

These agents of disruption make the necessary time or space in their lives to be able to commit to participating in God's justice work.

We've discussed the isolation, busyness, and unhealthy patterns of thinking that often prevent us from living this kind of life, but underlying them all is our understanding of prioritizing with intentionality. It's when we fail to understand this concept and don't take the steps necessary to modify our lives that we end up busy but not necessarily influential.

Experts and theorists agree that most of us desire to find meaning in our lives and do so by pursuing and embracing activities like raising children, positively developing our careers, or becoming active citizens who devote time to meaningful projects. In a 2019 study by the University of Alberta, researchers set out to replicate the findings of earlier studies on generativity, a sensation that was first described by the theorist Erik Erikson. Erikson believed humans have an internal desire to make an impact on future generations by contributing to the world. In the 2019 study, researchers found that "like intrinsically rewarding work, civic engagement provides the opportunity for people to become generative through helping others and contributing to society."[2]

The words of Scripture support this notion of generativity. Jesus said that he came into the world so that we may have life—and have it abundantly (see John 10:10). He advises us to fill our lives with spiritual riches: those that can be found when we pursue the work of God (see Matthew 6:20). Yet, if this is the kind of life to which we've all been called—and, indeed, that we so desire—then why is it so difficult for us to achieve? Most of us would cite a lack of time as the reason for our being unable to participate in meaningful activities. We live our lives routinely, showing up to work each day, running errands, taking care of kids (if we have them), getting together with friends over a meal, and making time for entertainment of some kind. We do all of these things without stopping to ask ourselves if the way in which we're living is really the way that we want to be living.

At some point, many of us question the monotony of our routine. Sadly, though, most of us will never dig deeper within ourselves to find the answer to the question of meaning. We dismiss the feeling as something with which all humans must struggle, and then get back to our normal routines, choosing to adhere to them because they're comfortable.

But what if we chose not to dismiss our feelings of dissatisfaction and instead really committed to creating a life full of meaning and purpose? The path that we choose to follow is ultimately up to each of us.

My friend Jimmy Starnes is an executive coach who regularly helps people fill their lives with more purpose. Jimmy thinks the notion of a lack of time in relation to undertaking meaningful activities is a myth.[3] He has found that the major problem for most people is that they fail to live with a central focus in mind and instead allow their days to be dictated by things that they believe to be out of their control. This leaves them with no time to even notice what's happening in their communities, let alone become involved. Jimmy helps people by first asking them to decide for what they'd like to be remembered and in what they would most like to invest. These two questions are what leads a person to take control of their schedule and create margin. Having margin is what allows us to discover our true purpose: to come up with creative ideas and to serve well.

Vanessa Howard creates margin in her busy schedule of running the Giving Hands Beauty Salon by dedicating one day each month to women who are experiencing homelessness or are the survivors of abuse. Having experienced homelessness herself, Vanessa believed that she'd been given a vision from God to help women like herself in Tampa, Florida.[4] So when she opened the salon in 2014, she began offering free makeovers once a month, bringing hope in the form of beauty as well as a copy of the Bible in a gift bag.[5] The salon is able to provide these monthly makeovers largely because of a team of volunteers that includes Vanessa's daughters as well as others. Vanessa has even been fortunate enough to see the women who have visited the salon go on to find employment.

Vanessa created the necessary space in her life and her business to give back to a community that desperately needs support. We sometimes fool ourselves into thinking that the people who do significant things to help others in life are somehow "special" or better-suited to the role of doing something big for their communities—but that's a lie. We can all do our part to seek justice together, but we must be willing to restructure our lives so that they do not reflect a comfortable routine but rather the values in which we claim to believe.

HOW TO CREATE MARGIN IN YOUR SCHEDULE

We are husbands, wives, fathers, mothers, brothers, sisters, sons, daughters, and employees, and balancing all of these roles is a challenge for everyone. So as you move forward with your work in community, you'll want to consider new tools and resources to help you incorporate the fight for justice into your life and to effect the logistical changes that are necessary to make it work for the long-term. If we do not prepare by adopting new scheduling habits, recruiting help, and communicating well with our loved ones, our first steps toward service can end up leading to conflict in our personal lives. Serving in the community should be an opportunity to offer your skills and your expertise—but never at the expense of your own self-care or your responsibilities to your family. I want to help you create a life that successfully supports your involvement in serving.

In order to schedule effectively, we must provide ourselves with the necessary mental space to figure out how to leverage our gifts for the betterment of others. The problem is that we typically don't allow ourselves that kind of room to think—not in a multitasking culture in which we pride ourselves on having an abundance of things to do each day. It is often when we afford our minds a bit of time to wander that our best ideas arise.

A writer friend of mine recently told me that she felt more mentally and spiritually healthy in the middle of a global pandemic than she had before. She and her husband normally lead such busy lives, she explained, that she often felt a tightness in her chest at random moments throughout the day. A low-grade anxiety that she didn't realize was brought on by busyness had been lifted by a decrease in being "on the go" all of the time. Though her workload is at an all-time high, she somehow feels freer than she ever has, and finds herself participating in hobbies around the house that have previously felt only like chores. She says, "I had started to believe that I hated being in my kitchen. But during this quieter season, I've realized that I only hated it because it was yet another thing to do during the day. I was in go-mode all the time. I realize now that I actually love it, when I don't have to do it at warp speed." Even in a season of complete uncertainty, she found a level of peace because she was able to breathe again.

Many of us find quiet time to be a luxury that we can't afford. I believe such time is a necessity. Jesus himself withdrew to quiet places of solitude in order to commune with the Father to seek direction—and he had every power under heaven at his fingertips. Moreover, if anyone had responsibilities and people depending upon him, it was Jesus—and yet he took time away by himself. In Matthew

14, for example, we see what I can only imagine as an emotionally spent Jesus retreat to a mountain to pray by
himself. His cousin and friend, John the Baptist, had just
been murdered, and immediately following that, Jesus is
feeding five thousand people. But verse 23 says, "And after
he had dismissed the crowds, he went up the mountain by
himself to pray. When evening came, he was there alone."

Jesus needed replenishment from his Father in heaven,
so it should be no surprise that we do too. Time for reflection, contemplation, and communion with God is ultimately where we receive clarity on all aspects of our lives,
including where we are most needed to serve in the work
of God. In his book *The Ruthless Elimination of Hurry*, John
Mark Comer offers the following perspective about Jesus
being led into the wilderness to be tempted by the devil: "It
was only after a month and a half of prayer and fasting in
the quiet place that he had the capacity to take on the devil
himself and walk away unscathed. That's why over and over
again you see Jesus come back to the eremos."[6]

Erēmos is a Greek word meaning "a desolate place." And
it's this kind of place that Jesus came back to in order to
commune with God. Then he came away strengthened and
ready to begin his ministry. The time that we give ourselves
for this same kind of deep reflection or prayer is what pre-
pares us for our own ministry or social justice work. Some
people believe in taking a traditional sabbath while others
schedule breaks that look more like a vacation at the end
of a work cycle. Either way, this time for our spiritual

health is a necessary break that allows ideas to flow and rest to occur before facing the effects of burnout.

Our strategies for scheduling margin should involve both long-term and short-term goals. For example, I plan for family vacations at least a year in advance of taking them. That way, I'm not scrambling for empty space in the calendar once it begins to fill up each year. Planning this far in advance may seem to be intense, but these are the kinds of proactive habits that have allowed my family and me to be very much involved in social justice work while still making time for one another. We have made intentionality part of our strategy to free ourselves up to do God's work alongside others. This is how we have the margin to stand with others around us.

I also schedule in priorities that need to occur more regularly before placing anything else on the calendar. My wife and I have been happily married for nearly fifteen years now. I believe that this is due in large part to our commitment to consistently having a date night each week. It's a non-negotiable opportunity for us to have quality time together. I recognize, however, that not everyone has the flexibility to be able to do this once per week with their spouse. And the goal is not a specific amount of time as much as it is overall health and time to connect with family. Often our dates are not anything elaborate—perhaps going for a walk or sitting on the porch with one another in order to find time for prolonged conversation once our kids are in bed. Maybe your date is a workout together at the gym or whatever fits your daily rhythm. The key is to create daily, weekly, monthly, and even quarterly rhythms.

One tool that's been helpful for me in creating this rhythm is what I call a "Life Map." This strategy breaks up each day into blocks and allows me to schedule which tasks make the most sense to be completed during a certain block. I even created a quarter map that helps me plan out several months at a time and a strategic year plan of high-level things that I want to accomplish and learn throughout the year. However, with the part of the Life Map that focuses on the week-to-week stuff, I usually look at the day in four-hour blocks. Having this type of view of the week helps me to realize what bests fits where. For example, I like to get my administrative tasks done during the block of time right after breakfast and before lunch. Then there is another block of time that occurs between lunch and dinner, and so on. I prioritize my family in the evenings, so during the block of time after dinner, I do not take any calls unless I have previously discussed and agreed to do so with my wife. You can see in the table what it looks like and a few questions that I ask myself each week.

What I also realize, however, is the flexibility I have as the leader of a nonprofit organization. Many people don't have the ability to set their own hours the way that I have been able to in recent years. When our work schedules are fixed, being intentional with the remainder of our hours

BREAKFAST: *What are the things you do best in the morning?*

SUNDAY	MONDAY	TUESDAY	WEDNESDAY	THURSDAY	FRIDAY	SATURDAY

LUNCH: *What are the things you do best after you have eaten or have shifted to post-morning activities?*

SUNDAY	MONDAY	TUESDAY	WEDNESDAY	THURSDAY	FRIDAY	SATURDAY

DINNER: *What are things you prefer to do in the evenings to help you unwind as the day comes to a close?*

SUNDAY	MONDAY	TUESDAY	WEDNESDAY	THURSDAY	FRIDAY	SATURDAY

will require boundaries as well, but they'll look different. Instead of blocking time during the weekday, you may be extra intentional with the way you spend your off-time. When I was working a traditional nine-to-five job as well as trying to get our nonprofit off the ground, I had to really rely on accountability from my family and friends to keep me intentional. For example, Saturdays were my family day. It meant that for at least four to five hours, my family would get my undivided attention. Accountability in my social circle was also important. My small group members became not only the people I was engaging in God's Word with, but also the people I served and socialized with.

No matter what kind of work we do, as we involve ourselves in the good and hard work of social justice, we'll have to adopt these kinds of boundaries to help protect and maintain healthy relationships with others. Likely hard conversations will need to happen with your loved ones regarding the sacrifices that your family can realistically make. For example, my wife and I have had to decide which one of us would go back to school for graduate degrees. Both of us? One of us? Could the other spouse's job support the family's need for health insurance? Intentional shifts toward following our callings cannot happen without transparent conversations within the home.

Below, you'll find a list of questions that will help you think through important decisions regarding your schedule. They'll also serve you in your ability to communicate scheduling shifts and changes to the most important people in your life:

- Does this activity take me away from my established intent or mission? If yes, then it's "mission creep," meaning it's potentially crowding out established priorities.

- If I add this activity or appointment to my plate, will it cause me to feel overwhelmed or burdened? If the answer is yes, you may want to say no to something that would potentially drain you.

- Does this activity align with my core values and intentions? Our core values can definitely serve as guardrails as to what we choose to involve ourselves in on a continuous basis.

- Is this something that I want to commit to temporarily or long-term? Weighing the length of commitment from a thirty-foot view can help us make critical decisions as to what we choose to pursue.

TRANSITIONING TO A LIFE OF PURPOSE

Most of us want to be remembered for the impact that we have made on the world, but it's also clear that we often pass up what's meaningful for something lesser. My intention is not to offend you with what I'm about to say—but I do intend to make you think hard about the kind of service in which you involve yourself and whether it keeps you from deeper interactions. Our service to God and our communities cannot be undertaken solely within the confines of a church. When we spend countless hours preparing the church bulletins or putting up decorations for events without giving a thought to the people outside of the church who are suffering, there is a problem not only with our priorities but also with the way in which we view our mission as Christians.

Dr. Will Gravely is on a mission to change the way his congregants view serving by changing the narrative around how church members give financially. Though he believes in the biblical mandate to tithe, he also believes that it should be a starting point for giving, not an endpoint. He says about his church culture,

> I removed tithing language from our culture. In the Bible, the tithe went to the work of the widow and the stranger. What does that look like in our culture? The orphan had no inheritance to receive. The widow had no inheritance to receive from the husband. The stranger could not enter the marketplace and do commerce. That's why God took care of people like that. Why would we just focus on the principle and not getting to the sick? At some churches, 90 percent of tithing is used for in-house bills. I don't want our church to pass a person in need trying to give their gift to God—that's what it's [your money] for. Helping congregants reframe their thinking and create a lifestyle of generosity is one profound way to help create

a culture of intentional living both in regards to money and time. How our church communities choose to utilize their financial means says a lot about where our hearts are. I've been a part of churches that were barely keeping the doors open because their own community was suffering financially, and they became caretakers for one another. If a child needed clothes, somebody stepped up and brought clothes. If a family needed a meal, another household would share. We raised funds, tithes, and offerings and used them to help pay bills and cover groceries. These were insulated acts of loving one another.

I've seen more affluent churches sport lights, cameras, smoke, fancy new clothes, and tons of resources, but no one was thinking about people outside of the church. Sometimes these churches are in metropolitan areas that are gentrified and benefiting from the displacement of other people. Being cognizant of this could have allowed them to be a blessing in these communities, lending a hand of fellowship and support to their neighbors.

These days, unfortunately, some of the most transformative acts done to help restore the image of God in someone happen outside of a church building. Once upon a time, during the civil rights era, the church gave direction to those who were lost and hurting and seeking justice. Pastors and ministers were often the people giving direction for social demonstrations. Yet today, I have pastors calling me to receive guidance on how to even approach the conversation of racism. I understand that many may disagree with me on this point, but I believe the church must begin linking arms far more often with outside organizations in order to best participate in healing. I'll be the first to acknowledge that the church has something unique to offer because it is representative of the divine God, but the church has also been tragically late in responding to injustices. The fact that many in the church still need convincing that racism even exists is delaying the work that could be taking place. After all, the church is not a building or a place; it is a group of people sharing God's news of love to the rest of the world. Why would we separate ourselves from sharing that love in parts of society that are doing tangible work?

Asking yourself what kind of work really matters to you will make it easier and easier to prioritize and create the margin you need to do that meaningful work. And as your life takes on new purpose and drive, you'll find that God will begin to use you as a catalyst for those you know to find their purpose as well. In the meantime, what can you do today to help prioritize your purpose? Only by choosing to live intentionally are you able to make yourself available and join in the company of others to seek justice together.

CHAPTER NINE

BRING SOMEONE
WITH YOU!

I was introduced to church as a kid by my grandmother, Jessica Lester. In fact, she's the reason that I was exposed to church at an early age. She had tremendous faith and made sure that I was around godly things when I was about eight years old when my dad was in prison. However, those concepts were very hard for me to grasp, and my childhood faith was based on needing to get things right. I never fully understood what it meant that God was full of grace and loved me even when I messed up. As I grew, my search for identity was cloudy, and I succumbed to many social pressures. I joined a gang, was rebellious, sold drugs, dropped out of high school for a time, ran away as a teenager, and even ended up in jail once after committing a small crime so I could party with my college friends. Fortunately, a judge decided to show me latitude when my mother begged him to let me go home. I can remember his words even now. He said, "This is the only chance you're getting. I see the pain your mom is in and the worry in her eyes. You need to get right and never look back." This is the same judge who was notorious for giving young Black men long sentences.

I never did look back.

God used that day to cause me to remember all of the lessons my grandmother tried to teach me as a child. Not long after moving back home from college to start over, I received a phone call from my childhood friend Harvey that changed the trajectory of my life. Harvey and I had grown up similarly, each of us having family challenges and searching for identity. But when we were both in our twenties, Harvey found his identity in God. One day, after he'd only attended his new church a few times, he called me. I was lost. I had just gotten out of a jail and had my charges dropped. He extended an invitation to come with him to church. I remember having some reservations about going, but I also knew that I needed something. So I found myself in church with Harvey that next week.

The pastor preached from Romans, and I listened as he talked about Jesus dying for me while I was still a sinner. The verse that he read was this: "But God demonstrates his own love for us in this: While we were still sinners, Christ died for us" (Romans 5:8 NIV). Before that moment, I had never understood the true, unconditional love of God. That good news would shape the rest of my life's work. The gospel message is what has fueled my desire to influence the lives of others for good, showing God's grace and mercy to those who have often never experienced it. Love Beyond

Walls might have never existed had Harvey not decided to follow that nudge to ask me to attend a small Bible study with him.

Our efforts don't have to be grandiose to have a profound impact. Harvey dialed my number and then sat next to me; that's it. He had only been back in church for a short time. He didn't know all the answers to the questions of Christianity, nor did he hold a master's degree in theology. He only knew that I was struggling, lost, and in much pain from the journey in my life. He also knew I had the potential to be someone great. He was just being the community that I needed. And he communicated this simple but much needed truth with his actions—he was there with me and so was God the whole time. It still brings tears to my eyes because his invitation changed my life, and Harvey is still working alongside me twenty-plus years later at Love Beyond Walls. We can all extend an invitation to people to come with us to serve in order to benefit their lives and because we believe they'll benefit the lives of others. Whether we're inviting them to church or to join us at another kind of organization, a simple invitation can have monumental effects.

FORGET ABOUT BEING AN EXPERT

It's important to educate ourselves on issues of injustice, but a lack of understanding about every nuance shouldn't keep us from entering into the fight or from inviting others into it. In order to work for justice, we need to possess a willingness to collaborate with others and to learn from them as we navigate new issues or begin to volunteer for an organization. We rarely have everything figured out when God asks us to embark on a task. Rather, he encourages all of us to become part of what he is already doing, right alongside others who are figuring it out as they go too.

There's an insidious voice that whispers to us, constantly reminding us that we're either incapable of taking the steps needed to pursue our ideas or that what we have in mind is simply too difficult to accomplish. But the Bible shows us that this is a lying voice. I'm reminded that the early disciples had no special skills that made them stand out to Jesus. He chose regular, ordinary fishermen like Peter and Andrew to be his disciples—men who possessed no unique talents that would have qualified them for ministry. What they had was a willingness to be led by him. In the Old Testament, God acted through Rahab, a woman who worked as a prostitute and who consequently would have been considered by most to be unworthy for God's work. He often chose people who were not of high status or fame to carry out his work; their abilities manifested themselves in their bravery and in their dependence upon God. Advocating on behalf of the poor requires no expertise, and neither does showing mercy to a condemned woman or giving to an orphan or a widow.

Theologian K. A. Ellis explains that the term *widow* in biblical times would have been applicable to many people who needed serving. A widow, in the biblical context, is a woman who is bereft of what a husband or family could provide. She explained,

It's her condition that scripturally qualifies her as a widow, not the circumstance that led her to that condition. The circumstance that left her bereft in a male-dominated may have been divorce, abandonment, death, imprisonment, being placed in a nursing home and forgotten, becoming physically or mentally disabled, being rejected by her family because of her faith, having been single and never married. The circumstances can be many and varied.[1]

By this definition, so many whom we meet are living the life of a "widow." We need not wait to be an expert to see them and serve them. Similarly, by this definition, the category of people who need help is far too large for us to be able to tackle alone. We must bring people with us. More often than not though, we'll have to help them push through the false idea of their own deficiency as well.

LOOK FOR PARTNERS

The experience of bringing others along with us is one of the most exciting parts of the adventure. This is when we get to say, "We stand together in this work." However, the problem is that many people whom you know are still in the place where you once were: a place of believing that they lack the necessary skills or understanding to be able to participate.

I remember feeling similarly when I was a young man going to the recreation center to play pick-up basketball games. What would start off as casual fun always evolved into a scenario in which small teams would be formed, captains would be chosen, and a selection process would commence. For those of us who were on the sidelines, it was grueling, silently wondering whether we were good enough to be chosen and what the captains thought of our abilities.

Feelings like that are broadly experienced by people who are waiting to be seen and recognized for what they have to offer society. But yet again, I'm reminded of Jesus' approach to getting people to join the work that he was undertaking: he was invitational. He specialized in showing people that they were worthy. When he sees Simon and Andrew casting their net into the sea, he says to them, "Follow me and I will make you fish for people" (Mark 1:17). He saw what they were already involved in on one level and invited them in to play at a much deeper one, with more impact.

The story reminds me of my friend Kevin, who fell in love with serving the local homeless community in California after volunteering once during a health fair put on by his church. What began as shaving the heads of men who came in wanting a haircut evolved into a more holistic approach to caring for the community. As a personal trainer, when Kevin's clients first sign up for training, he lets them know that a portion of their fees will be donated to a local shelter for the homeless, and he also invites them to join him in volunteering on the last Saturday of every month. This results in him routinely bringing clients with him to serve meals and set up free pop-up clothing stores. Additionally, he offers a stretching ministry for those suffering from the aches and pains of living on the streets. Kevin says,

> I let my clients know that they have the opportunity to be a part of something bigger than just exercise. I think when I talk about my joy in doing it, then it sounds enjoyable to them too. And if someone arrives for their workout with a bag of clothes to donate, I always challenge them to come with me and actually give away that donation themselves. That way they can experience actually giving it to someone who needs it. And experience the impact that they can have.

Kevin has had the opportunity to bring people along with him who may have been too afraid of the unknown to ever actually go to a shelter alone, but who had a desire to make things right in the world. The invitation just needed to be extended and a vision had to be cast. As we move into a life of justice work, part of our job is to become vision casters.

CAST A VISION

An important component of our relationships with others should be our dedication to helping people identify their gifts. This is not solely so that they realize their potential in serving but rather so that they realize their potential *period*. When we see them exhibiting gifts like cooking, organizing, planning, singing, writing, communicating, speaking, praying, artistry, or an understanding of technology, we need to begin to cast a vision—that is to say, we need to help them see their own potential for serving at their fullest capacity within a community. Any of us can get a vision for ourselves and others to serve in practical ways.

Harvey had only been to his church a handful of times before inviting me to join him; he saw that I needed a place that offered my life hope. Kevin only served at the shelter for the homeless once before deciding to return on a regular basis. You can help cast a vision by inviting others to events that will help them see the kind of work that is already being undertaken for the good of society and on behalf of the individuals who are in greatest need. People need to see where they fit within the larger picture. Paint that picture—showing them where the holes are situated—and you'll be surprised how people will step up to offer their time and resources as a result.

For example, Sam is one of our volunteers. A friend invited him to do some volunteer work for his first time, and Sam has since become one of our greatest volunteers. Sam went from volunteering once to literally showing up every single week to help us lead a food co-op for community members that are food insecure. When I asked Sam what made him show up every single week, he simply said, "I have always wanted to get involved, but nobody ever gave me an opportunity." Although Sam doesn't think what he does is huge, it has a huge effect when elderly people see his smile and are greeted by him. He reminds people that they matter to God and to him. Every little bit counts.

Most people automatically downplay the extent to which they already help others because it doesn't seem to be as flashy as the work that they've seen politicians, CEOs, or other high-status individuals undertaking in the media. But the example of Sam is the type of everyday story that reminds us that we can all do our part—no matter our status. It's true: ensuring that extra food is being distributed to children is not going to solve the deeper systemic issues of why those children's families don't have enough food in the first place. However, when each of us does our part, we are able to provide relief and to show compassion to others; this is no small thing in itself. In lending our support, we are letting people know that they are seen as living, breathing humans who are worthy and who deserve dignity. Some people will write policy, some will run for office, and some will make calls, while others will write petitions, deliver food, provide shelter and groceries, and a host of other things that make one large tapestry of social change. It is all needed.

Each and every one of us has something unique to offer and an important part to play in the mission to bring justice to the world. When describing the value found in all spiritual gifts, the apostle Paul offers an analogy of our physical bodies, pointing to the fact that each of our body parts is dependent upon another and that not a single one is without value (1 Corinthians 12:14-20).

We are all equipped to do *something*. No, we are not all meant to teach the incarcerated or to crochet blankets for children who are suffering from terminal diseases. Those things do need to be done; someone has been made specifically to offer such acts of mercy and grace. It is when we all function in our own areas of expertise and passion that the most effective work can be undertaken, both in the workplace and in the community. Channeling our skills, talents, and passions into meaningful acts ensures that we give in a spirit of sincerity that is obvious to those whom we're seeking to help. And it allows us to embrace our roles as natural assets to any organizations to whom we give our time and expertise.

When Sam was given an opportunity, it revealed to him the ways in which he could contribute to make the world better. Sometimes people just need exposure to issues that they can fight for. Similar to another friend who participated in helping people register to vote for the first time in the state of Georgia to help fight voter suppression. When people are invited, God shows them what areas or gaps they can fill.

The great thing about this is that invitations create more invitations and allows people to also invite their friends out to help them contribute in greater ways.

SHARE THE WEIGHT

Preparing individuals to enter into either our work or the area of service about which they are most excited helps to bring new energy to any mission. It's also what's most needed for the health of those who are already contributing to the cause. For leaders who have been serving for some time, the problem is not one of believing they can make a difference, but rather believing that there are others who would like to help them make that difference, and help carry the weight. It's when leaders forget to invite people to join them in the work that they face burnout.

With packed schedules and concentration strictly focused on righting the wrongs of this world, those who consistently find themselves in a helping role to those who are experiencing trauma can become susceptible to what's called "vicarious trauma." This is when our closeness to someone else's severe hardship begins to color our own thoughts, emotions, and behaviors—almost as if the helper has experienced the trauma too. Activists as well as many others in professions that come into close contact with traumatic situations can experience this. Though it can be an occupational hazard for those who have direct involvement in a crisis, there are strategies that can help ease stress in other areas of life.

Jason Fried and David Heinemeier Hansson's book *Rework,* for example, helped me look at the external pressures that compound my own fatigue as a leader.[2] They talk about learning what your capacity is, taking into account how much you're already involved in, and consequently recognizing your limits. As a leader in social justice, I have often had to remind myself that these deep societal problems that we're working to eliminate will not go away overnight, and the issues of racism and of people being seen as less than human are ones that have been with us for centuries and will take years and years of work to eradicate. And we have to do it together, not alone.

We also need to remind ourselves often that our work does matter, and things *do* happen. For example, after Breonna Taylor was tragically killed in March 2020 by police officers, the large public outcry led to significant reform at the city level. The "no-knock" search warrant that allowed officers entry into Breonna's home without any identification was banned in Louisville. Also included in that proposed legislation, dubbed Breonna's Law, is a mandate that all officers must wear body cameras whenever a warrant is being served.[3]

Although the police officers that claimed the life of Breonna Taylor were not charged, it has motivated a community to fight to end these types of warrants that end in the killing of Black and Brown bodies. The public demanded that officers no longer be able to enter a citizen's home without identifying themselves, and justice leaders lent their own voices to advocate for Breonna's family by using their social media platforms and influence to speak about it. People, regardless of their social status, income, resources, or age, can seek justice together and make change!

When we understand this, we can more effectively prepare the next generation for service as we look again for others to help carry the weight. We have unlimited power when we find and include others who can join us in the fight. As a Black man in America, the way in which I look at any given social justice issue is different from how a twentysomething Mexican American woman might look at the very same issue, just as an eighty-year-old Asian American man will have his own entirely different perspective. Let's be clear again that diversity means we invite people to the table while inclusion empowers voices to be heard and embraced while individuals are at the table. As I stated earlier, diversity that is not empowering is simply shallow marketing. Ultimately, it's inclusion that leads to better, more equitable communities.

INVITE PEOPLE INTO COMMUNITY

Finding others for the fight cannot be a one-strategy mission. By that, I mean that our eyes should be trained to see the gifts of not only our friends, family, or coworkers but also those whom we serve. As we forge and develop connections with those who are living in poverty, we should not limit our understanding of such individuals by seeing them solely as people who require care; rather, we should ensure that we also think of them as people who have something meaningful to contribute to the community. In Asset-Based Community Development, for example, the idea is to look for strengths within a community in order to empower the community itself. The model puts the citizens in the driver's seat in serving other citizens, as opposed to looking to outside institutional help, which may be excessive and can lower the ability of the community themselves to serve one another.

Richard Miles is helping former prison inmates understand that they are worthy of being part of a community. He provides these men and women with the resources they need in order to find jobs and get their lives back on track. Richard himself endured fifteen years—of a sixty-year sentence—in prison for a crime that he did not commit. While he was an inmate, Richard noticed how often people returned to prison following their release because they lacked the skills that they needed to successfully reintegrate into their communities. Therefore, in the years after his release, Richard got to work by launching Miles of Freedom: a nonprofit organization that empowers men and women who were formerly incarcerated to find jobs and to become fully functioning members of their communities. Though his organization provides tangible resources such as assistance with securing identification or writing résumés, Richard believes that one of the most important gifts given to these men and women is building up their confidence. He says to his students, "At the end of the day, be confident in your change."[4]

The empowerment, the affirmation of the dignity of *all* people, is that which makes a true community. It is that which helps every member to flourish.

Pamela Barba is helping lift up her community in this way as well. She and her organization, Vamos Ladies, has been addressing the justice issue of the wage gap for Latinx communities since 2017. They provide resources for Latina entrepreneurs that include business and branding advice as well as one-on-one coaching. The organization's assistance for women with a dream of building their own businesses is a part of her larger mission to "increase wealth . . . in Latinx communities."[5] Helping Latinas get the skills they need to bring their dreams to fruition is helpful to the Latinx community and beyond. For it's only when we are all operating at our highest level that an entire community and nation can really thrive. More people having a sense of safety and security and the ability to provide for their families makes for a stronger and more vibrant society, as does having a place where everyone has your best interests at heart and in mind.

From the very beginning of the world's creation, we can see that God has been calling us to work toward the creation of a true community with him: "And God blessed them. And God said to them, 'Be fruitful and multiply and fill the earth and subdue it, and have dominion over the fish of the sea and over the birds of the heavens and over every living thing that moves on the earth'" (Genesis 1:28 ESV). The truth, however, is that for many people, this type of healthy community is elusive. Having felt marginalized since they were young, and perhaps living just a few streets away from us, they may have never experienced the kind of societal acceptance that is enjoyed by the dominant culture. They may never have had the opportunity to live with the same privilege of feeling free and accepted. This

could be due to the color of their skin, their sexual orientation, or their immigration status. They are used to experiencing feelings of danger—not security. Imagine the
impact that such feelings would have on a person over
time. Insecurity can be a major contributing factor to an
individual's inability to make meaningful relational connections, secure a good job, support themselves, and find
resources in their communities.

What would it look like if every person were given an
equal chance to succeed and to show up as a fully accepted
member of society? This is the real essence of social justice:
the pursuit of a society that welcomes each and every
person and draws them into a community that is excited
about what they have to contribute. Jesus extended an invitation to everyone he came across, no matter their social
standing, because he knew that they had all been made in
the image of God. Indeed, he did so to such an extent that
he was criticized for it by those who didn't understand
God's intention to restore *all* people.

Challenge yourself to think about the people you know,
and catalog the skills of your friends, family, and coworkers.
Then begin to cast a vision for each of them. Let them know
that you see them.

CHAPTER TEN

MAXIMIZE YOUR IMPACT

As we've looked at our need to emerge from isolation in order to work for justice within our society, it's important that we look at how isolation affects those we seek to serve. A very real sense of isolation accompanies poverty. This is in part because a lack of financial means decreases opportunities for social connectedness, causing another kind of poverty: social poverty. The factors that bring about this lack of social connectedness include things like not having a job; being employed typically enables us to see our coworkers regularly and get to know them in more depth. It also widens our social circle. Those who do not have regular opportunities to connect with people who know and love them—or to meet anyone new, for that matter—struggle greatly with social poverty. And the problem is undoubtedly exacerbated by the fact that the places at which we prefer to gather tend to cost us money.

When we encounter a homeless encampment, I believe that what we're seeing is not only an attempt to secure a feeling of safety but also a way of curbing the loneliness that characterizes life on the streets. We need to be willing to serve not just in the traditional sense of volunteering or activism but also in the sense of inviting people into a community by offering forms of real companionship. We need to reach out to those who are routinely forgotten.

There is a growing body of evidence to support the notion that human beings are hardwired to desire—and, indeed, need—connection. In her book *Daring Greatly*, Brené Brown talks about connection in relation to her definition of "Wholehearted living," which she defines as "engaging in our lives from a place of worthiness."[1] Brené goes on to say that a fundamental component of this definition is the idea that "love and belonging are irreducible needs of all men, women, and children. We're hardwired for connection—it's what gives purpose and meaning to our lives. The absence of love, belonging, and connection always leads to suffering."[2]

Saying that we're "hardwired" for connection is another way of saying that human beings can only function properly when our need for interaction with others is being fulfilled. We were not made to live in isolation but rather with people who can help carry our burdens and offer us comfort—and with those to whom we can give such things in return.

Discussions about prospective solutions to the homeless crisis in America often lead to conversations about mental health and the lack of necessary resources. However, I wonder how often we stop to think about the impact that forming simple social connections could have on an individual within a marginalized group of people, whether it be those who are suffering from mental illness or even those who are plagued by drug and alcohol addictions. Humans are complex beings who need more than just health services to treat their symptoms of illness and unhappiness. We also need to have heart-to-heart conversations and connections. So, as we look to provide "wraparound" services—like mental and physical health resources—we should also provide social connections. As people who seek to be servants, we cannot build communities for ourselves that don't include those who look different from us, have a different level of health than we do, or make a different amount of money than we do. We must widen our circles if we ever hope to make the type of impact that goes farther than merely superficial help. Connections are what change people from the inside out.

Without our intentional efforts, these social connections are hard to come by for most people who wonder if they belong in the first place. Making time to form these connections can be seen as an inconvenience or the last priority after the things we do for our own benefit. But a life of faith should never place us at the center. This is exactly where many of us find ourselves, however— serving ourselves and people who are just like us. At the same time, we see society continuing to push impoverished people farther and farther away from everything that constitutes normalcy. When people do not have jobs, money for entertainment, a car to get them from point A to point B, clean clothes to wear to a public meeting place like a coffee shop, or the energy or money that is needed to join a gym or to take a class, and no one wants to see a shelter being built in their neighborhood . . . what's left? People are completely bereft of opportunities for meaningful connections with others.

I recently came across a photograph on social media that was deeply disturbing. It was an image of a cement ledge outside a store in the middle of a city. The ledge—on which an individual could, ordinarily, easily sit for a few moments—was covered in spikes. Not the kind of spikes that are meant to drive away birds, but larger ones—ones meant to drive away humans. I did a bit of digging and found that the picture was an example of "hostile architecture": a phrase being used to describe design elements that are meant to prevent people from congregating or resting.[3] This is not an approach that stops at spikes. The design elements can be more subtle, like a slanted bench, which obviously makes it impossible for an individual to sleep on. And there are plenty more examples of this kind of design, like benches being removed from subway stations or the partial coverage of vents, which keeps public areas from being as well-heated in colder months.

We are telling *people*—every day, with our words or through our actions—that they are unwanted. Just think for a moment about the idea of placing spikes on a surface to keep people from sitting. Aren't we communicating that their humanity is a nuisance? Like an animal being there might be a nuisance? When we punish people for attempting to sit, we are criminalizing them for being poor. And the sentiment behind that criminalization is at the core of every form of social injustice: that some people are worthy of good quality lives and some are not.

Urban sociologist Eric Klinenberg has devoted much thought to physical spaces and to the ways public meeting places could offer possible opportunities for connection— places like libraries, for example. He says that, as a nation, we're lacking social infrastructure, which he defines as the physical places that shape the ways in which we interact. More and more often, he explains, the "places that we used to congregate are closed," and "we pay to be a part of public life."[4] When I think of these public places, I think of the respite they used to offer for people who were without shelter, or the entertainment that a library provided for those who had no money for books or movies. Opportunities both to connect and to rest are being lost with the closure of every public space that has been deemed unprofitable.

This is what happened when our city closed one of the largest shelters in the city of Atlanta. The Peachtree-Pine shelter closed in August 2017 and right after the closing, it was reported that many people experiencing homelessness died from hypothermia.[5] Also, there is a neighborhood in a city of California that launched a campaign to raise resources to block the building of a homeless shelter. These San Franciscans raised seventy thousand dollars to stop a homeless shelter in a wealthy area.[6] It got so bad that a rival campaign was launched:

But it also spurred supporters of the shelter to try to beat them at their own game. Since launching on Thursday, a rival GoFundMe has amassed over $73,000. And it had drawn hefty contributions of $10,000 each from the Salesforce CEO Marc Benioff, the Twilio CEO Jeff Lawson, and from GoFundMe itself. The San Francisco resident who created it, William Fitzgerald, said that the dollars rolling in on the other side shocked him into action. "They clearly don't like people who don't have the same amount of money in their bank account as they do, they clearly don't like people who look different, who sleep outside at night."

Although this community had houses that averaged a worth of one million dollars, they wanted to block people from having a place to reside.

Eric's work to investigate how social infrastructure affects the poor actually started with his publication, *Heat Wave: A Social Autopsy of Disaster in Chicago,* in which he unpacks the tragic events that occurred during a Chicago heatwave in 1995 when over seven hundred people died.[7] In his investigation for the book, he discovered the role that isolation, fear, and poverty played in the shocking death rate. Tragically, many of these deaths were, in fact, preventable. A high number of people might have survived had they simply been connected to someone who could have checked on them regularly throughout the intense heat, invited them to their own home so that they could benefit from their air-conditioning, or else taken them to a public place that was cool, well-ventilated, and air-conditioned.[8]

CREATE CONNECTIONS

So what can we do as people who desire to improve our communities and, by extension, the world? We can do our best to lobby for these types of public meeting places to be kept open. The key concern, though, is not really the buildings or institutions themselves so much as the connection points that they provide for people who are alone. What if instead of people experiencing homelessness, not having access to shelter in the winter, or having a shelter blocked because they do not have access to wealth, we lobbied to ensure that people without an address are treated like neighbors. I often say in my talks that just because a person does not have an address does not mean that they aren't our neighbor.

The Bible reveals two key concepts within the first pages of Genesis that speak to the issue. The first is that we, as humans, have been made in his image, and therefore each and every one of us is worthy just by being alive. The second is perhaps even more telling. At the end of designing every aspect of creation, God looks down and calls it "good." God does not deem anything to be "bad," in fact, until Genesis 2:18 (ESV), when he sees the man alone and says: "It is not good that the man should be alone; I will make him a helper fit for him." From these verses, it stands to reason that our job as servants within a community is to help people understand their God-given worth and to provide both individual and group companionship.

I met the Andersons one Sunday when I was preaching about Jesus extending invitations to outsiders, and this couple was trying to do just that. They were on a mission to become proximate with people who were outside their normal circles. Their story stands out in my memory to this day because it so clearly illustrated the point that I had been trying to make in my sermon. The couple spoke about befriending an elderly homeless couple whose names were Marla and John. They had passed them in the park on their way to work each day. It was a story that was built on one connection after another, each of which had finally led to this elderly couple getting back on their feet.

The story began with the Andersons offering Marla and John a vacant rental property, free of charge, to live in temporarily. Then they rallied their small group to help find a job for John and, for Marla, the mental health counseling that she needed. This small team of people worked together to formulate a three-month plan that would help the couple be able to afford a longer stay at a boarding house. Essentially, they came together to serve this elderly couple in a way that communicated, "Hey, you're one of us and we're going to help you, in the same way that we would if you were a member of our own families or a close friend."

This is the kind of love that helps to diminish the feelings of loneliness and isolation and that lets people know they are truly welcome in our community.

For my friend Eryn Eddy, communicating this exact message meant using her personal hobby of spray-painting her own T-shirts with the phrase "So Worth Loving" for the benefit of others.[9] In 2011, Eryn was regularly blogging in an effort to get people to see how valuable they were, regardless of the struggles that they'd been through in their lives. Nine years later, she's selling a variety of products with her mantra that everybody is worth loving displayed across them. Even more impressive than that, though, is the belief behind the mission of So Worth Loving. Eryn says:

> The battle isn't are we worth loving. . . . The battle for us is to see clearly all the things that try to distract us from the truth that we already are worth loving. There is nothing we can do, no genetic predisposition, illness, or sin, that will separate us from our Creator. You are as is: worth loving.[10]

"So Worth Loving" is not just a catchy slogan but, rather, something that we all need to communicate to those who are alone and hurting, whether it's due to poverty, sexual orientation, race, chronic illness, or old age. Yes, we will continue to need policy changes in order to eliminate issues like wealth disparity, systemic racism, and unequal pay for minorities and women; it is just as important, though, that we come near to those who are suffering.

RECOGNIZE YOUR SOCIAL CAPITAL

Often we take our networks of friends and family for granted until we face some major inconvenience in our lives. For example, if my car breaks down suddenly, even if I wasn't able to afford a tow truck, I have a variety of people who are only one phone call away from coming to pick me up. Having a variety of people to help support you through life is called social capital. Take a moment to think about how much of it you have.

To whom, or what, would you turn if you had neither the financial means or social capital to assist you when you needed it? I recently spoke with a firefighter named Rick whose department was experiencing the brunt of a near epidemic of loneliness. They were receiving hundreds of repeat calls from people who were not actually experiencing emergency situations; they were, in fact, ringing with mundane problems that almost anyone would be able to help them with—if they had anyone in their lives, that is. The non-crisis calls were typically about things like having lost their keys or socks or having experienced minor falls, and they were made by people who were living in isolation in low-income homes and, often, were elderly. In some instances, the calls came from people who lived in impoverished neighborhoods where the electricity had been disconnected or the water had been turned off because they couldn't afford to pay the bill.

There wasn't much that Rick could do in his position; he had more traditional, pressing emergencies to which he needed to respond. But, having wrestled with what could be done, he settled on what sounds a lot like what the church traditionally calls "loving our neighbor." He wondered whether faith communities could set up a rotating system of individuals who would visit people who desperately needed connection. It would be relatively straightforward for a small group of people to get together to build—or to raise the funds for—a ramp outside a disabled or elderly person's home, he reasoned. And what about when the temperature dropped? Could churches provide a rotating network of shelters for those who were without a home?

The various ideas that Rick considered should not strike us as being novel or groundbreaking; they should be things that churches are already doing. Indeed, churches should be on the frontlines of people who are working to provide the social infrastructure that Eric Klinenberg described: places for connection that can heal the loneliness from which people are suffering. Writer and theologian Henri J. M. Nouwen said,

> Compassion challenges us to cry out with those in misery, to mourn with those who are lonely, to weep with those in tears. Compassion requires us to be weak with the weak, vulnerable with the vulnerable, and powerless with the powerless. Compassion means full immersion in the condition of being human.[11]

The Bible gives much the same direction to humans, saying, "Rejoice with those who rejoice, weep with those who weep" (Romans 12:15). Throughout Romans, the apostle Paul talks about Christian characteristics that believers should exemplify. Directly after issuing this call to rejoice and weep in community, he also says: "Live in harmony with one another. Do not be haughty, but associate with the lowly. Never be wise in your own sight" (Romans 12:16 ESV).

We've all found ourselves lonely at one time or another, and there is a common feeling of wanting to belong, no matter who we are. What's particularly interesting is that, according to research, most of us look for friends who are exactly like us. A 2018 Barna study found that, across every demographic—religion, race, income, level of education, social status, political view, and life stage—people overwhelmingly chose to become friends with people who were very similar to them.[12] Conventional wisdom would say that this makes sense, but the same study reported that one in five adults feels lonely even though they have a few close friends. So what's going on? Could it be that we're not here on this earth simply to congregate with our own kind of people but rather to live beyond the narrow parameters that we've placed upon our relationships? Could it be that our mission here is to multiply, not just in the sense of having children but also in terms of sharing the love of God with those who are unreached? I believe that Scripture corroborates the view that this is indeed our mission. Yet very few of us are living this way. In fact, the

most disturbing aspect of all of the research that was pre-
sented by Barna was this:

> Evangelicals are less likely than most to have friends
> who are different than them, especially when it comes
> to religious beliefs (91% mostly similar), ethnicity
> (88%), and political views (86%). As we've seen in
> other Barna research, friendship with those who are
> different to us increases empathy and causes a shift
> in our views toward them—in very positive ways.[13]

How does this reflect the call for Christians to live out-
wardly, reaching toward others who need a message of
hope and renewal? Truthfully, it doesn't. And unless people
of faith shift their perspectives on how to interact with
others and how to befriend individuals, I'm afraid that
these numbers won't change; what's more, the social injustices of today will continue. We will remain separated by
issues of race, sexual orientation, socioeconomic status,
age, and every other category that you can think of because we have yet to emerge from our bubbles of "sameness."
And we *all* will continue to experience the kind of loneliness that we feel because we are not living the way in
which we have been called to live.

The great news is that we can all start to live differently
at this very moment, becoming individuals who reach
out to those who are different in an effort to see them as
just another human being who has been made in the
image of God.

NEW WAYS TO GATHER

The value of making connections outside of our normal social circles is incalculable because of the way in which it opens up our minds and shows us that we're all humans who experience the same emotions. And relationships are key to our understanding of the very common desire that we all have: to feel safe, loved, and valued. They are the essence of what it means to say, "when we stand." An article in *The Atlantic* described the importance of relationships with this analogy:

> When economists put a price tag on our relationships, we get a concrete sense of just how valuable our social connections are—and how devastating it is when they are broken. If you volunteer at least once a week, the increase to your happiness is like moving from a yearly income of $20,000 to $75,000. If you have a friend that you see on most days, it's like earning $100,000 more each year. Simply seeing your neighbors on a regular basis gets you $60,000 a year more. On the other hand, when you break a critical social tie—here, in the case of getting divorced—it's like suffering a $90,000 per year decrease in your income.[14]

A framework that may help you think through your new mission—to multiply through connection—is to consider the places you frequent. There are more than likely people whom you've seen in those places before with whom you've never even spoken. There's the young woman who sits three chairs down from you in your classroom, for example, and the server in the restaurant at which you frequently stop for lunch. Then there's the cashier at the grocery store that you go to every single week. These might be people who are of a different race than you or who you may have once overheard espousing political views that are different from the ones that you hold. I'd challenge you to enter into conversation with them. Don't let such differences stop you. Say, "Hello. How are you?" And mean it. Wait for the answer and make a comment that invites an exchange. It does not have to be anything complex! It can be as simple as saying in return to the cashier, "Yes, it's been a busy day for me too. There was so much traffic on the way to get here, but I'm trying to get home in time to see . . ." Mention your favorite TV show here. The idea is not to create deep, meaningful dialogue from the start; the idea is to find connection points into which you can delve deeper as time goes on and you both become comfortable enough to converse with one another in more meaningful ways. Remember, you don't need to be an expert at anything! You just need to care.

This is by no means a solution to our societal problems, but it's a way to increase comfort with one another. The real solutions come once you've reached the stage at which you're inviting the folks whom you've met to gather. It could be that you mention to your restaurant server that you'd like to buy a meal for the homeless man who's sitting just outside. Perhaps you reference the fact that you also volunteer with an organization that serves the impover-ished and suggest that they check it out . . . In fact, they're welcome to join you the next time that you go. Opening doors to the next conversation—and then the next—is the place at which we have to begin.

If you're not someone who regularly talks to strangers, this is going to feel awkward at first. I understand that be-cause I'm naturally introverted myself. When I first started giving talks as part of my life as a pastor and activist, for example, I would feel nauseous before going onstage. I had to train myself to start thinking less about myself and how I'd be perceived and more about the message. But there are always ways that we can get our message across without being in the spotlight.

When we get comfortable talking to people whom we come across in our daily lives, we then slowly start to become comfortable with those whom we would perhaps never even have previously considered talking to. We might then begin to venture into other parts of the community, intentionally going out of our way to visit the grocery store on the other side of town or to research organizations in the area that are volunteering to clean up the neigh-borhood. When we get outside of ourselves and make con-nections that lead to the opening of hearts and minds, we maximize our impact.

CONCLUSION

PLAY YOUR PART

As I interacted with the local homeless population in my community during the global pandemic of 2020, it became obvious that many of them were starting to worry. What if quarantine orders meant that there was nowhere for them to stay? What if they had nowhere to wash their hands? I remember a man in his forties named Dimitri coming to me in tears because he was worried about what might happen to him. I knew that Love Beyond Walls had to offer some kind of help. We couldn't just leave people defenseless against Covid-19. But I was also unsure what we could really do. Our volunteer base had been dwindling rapidly, as had our donor base.

I remember sitting on the couch one night with my wife asking God what he wanted me to do. His answer came in the form of commercial after commercial proclaiming that the best defense against Covid-19 was the practice of washing one's hands frequently.

Well, what about the homeless? I thought.

LOVE SINKS IN

My question, in turn, prompted an idea: what if we were to provide portable sinks for the homeless? Suddenly remembering the RV units that had been donated to Love Beyond Walls by way of temporary housing for our community, I began to wonder whether we may be able to leverage the equipment from the RVs to produce portable sinks. *That'd be a start,* I thought. But we only had the makings of a few sinks.

Then my friend and hip-hop artist Lecrae decided to donate fifteen more. The day we installed those sinks, the story was captured by a media outlet. Suddenly, in the midst of a pandemic, global attention had been drawn to our project based in Atlanta. As the virus was beginning to spread, people were starting to recognize the very real need to keep all of us—regardless of socioeconomic status—safe. We began to feel hopeful, despite the crisis, as big businesses, organizations, and individuals such as Brawny, Hilton Foundation, Porsche, Ally Bank, Coca-Cola, UPS, Google, the NFL, AbbVie Inc., Katie Couric, and the Jeremy Lin Foundation reached out to partner with us, providing more sinks than we could have ever imagined.

Since launching the Love Sinks In campaign, we have expanded to more than fifty cities all around the United States, which means that each week, tens of thousands of people have access to this basic necessity that should be a permanent fixture in society. All because we choose to partner with others and seek justice alongside people who have a heart of togetherness.

RECOGNIZING OUR INTERCONNECTEDNESS

In the midst of the campaign, the world started to take an interest in helping the most impoverished members of society protect their health. Many people reached out to us for advice about how they might participate in the collective endeavor for the good of their own homeless communities. While I was encouraged by this newfound interest in the movement, I also found myself asking a question: Why did it take a global pandemic for people to decide to do something for those who have already been "socially distanced" and neglected for years?

Perhaps it was because, in the middle of a pandemic, people finally felt the extent of their own spiritual poverty. They were thus finally able to identify with the plight of those who are lonely—and do not have anyone to care for them—for the very first time. I guess that any major changes in our perspectives are almost always precipitated by a life-altering experience.

At times like these, when our interconnectedness as human beings is most apparent, I think back to the words that I wrote in *I See You: How Love Opens Our Eyes to Invisible People* regarding how we are all like parts of a garment, having been woven together:

> When a thread starts to unravel in a piece of clothing, the entire garment is threatened because the thread does not stand alone. The thread, although apparently isolated, is connected to the entire fabric. The owner of

the piece of clothing would be foolish to say, "Allow the thread to suffer because it's caused its own hardship." No, the owner would say, "let me care for the thread because it hurts that entire piece of clothing."[1]

If we consider God to be the designer of this garment and the sustainer of life, then we must also believe that he regards every thread as just as valuable as the next. And if we were to think of ourselves as common threads, we'd perhaps recognize our own importance in supporting the threads around us that are beginning to unravel. We must see ourselves as sources of support for each other. Scripture tells us to express our love for each other through action: "By this we know love, that he laid down his life for us, and we ought to lay down our lives for the brothers. But if anyone has the world's goods and sees his brother in need, yet closes his heart against him, how does God's love abide in him? Little children, let us not love in word or talk but in deed and in truth" (1 John 3:16-18 ESV).

BECOME ONE WHO LOVES
IN DEED AND TRUTH

Ms. Pam recognized her own standing as a common thread in the garment when she came to volunteer with our organization about two and a half years ago. Unlike her previous experiences of volunteering with the homeless, during her time with us, she was able to form relationships with those who may have been unlike her in terms of their economic status but who were similar to her in other ways.

They shared some of her desires, hopes, and hurts. Ms. Pam's encounters with those who were experiencing homelessness slowly began to influence how she felt about the homeless in general and brought about a complete shift in her perspective. Having once admitted that she felt slightly scared about the prospect of working with such individuals, she now saw them as fellow human beings and looked for ways in which she could serve them, even outside of her time volunteering with us.

Ms. Pam's new priority—to become proximate with others so that she might see and serve those in need— became as normal as any other routine that she had in her life. She was suddenly aware of all of the ways in which she could help those whom she passed at the gas station or elsewhere. She wasn't doing so because caring for people had become a trendy thing to do, nor was she simply following the latest fad in Christianity. Instead, Ms. Pam had simply come to see herself as a thread within the garment, and fellow men and women—regardless of their status or wealth—as threads in the garment as well. She had also learned that sharing God's love looks a lot like receiving all people: all those who have been created in God's image.

Father Greg Boyle first introduced me to the idea of "receiving" another human. Father Greg, of course, has been working for years with men and women who were formerly incarcerated and formerly in gangs to help them become productive citizens again. When I asked him how to best serve vulnerable communities, I remember the remarkably clear way in which he boiled everything down into simpler terms. It wasn't so much about serving, he explained, as it was about *receiving* people. He went on to break down the idea of the "other" and emphasized the fact that we are all *one*. This idea can also be found in Luke 9:48 (ESV), where Jesus calls his followers to understand that, by welcoming others, we are welcoming him: "Whoever receives this child in my name receives me, and whoever receives me receives him who sent me. For he who is least among you all is the one who is great."[2]

As opposed to seeing those whom we serve through an "I" and "you" perspective or an "us" and "them" lens, we should see everyone as being equal members of God's family. Regardless of our economic standing, none of us are fundamentally any different from one another. Therefore, our efforts to help impoverished individuals do not necessarily need to look any different from those that we adopt in order to support a loved one.

CHOOSE TO BECOME PART OF "US"

At times, I think that the word *serve* may do us all a disservice. Of course, the word in and of itself is not a bad one—but I think that it's one that immediately connotes ideas of separation and hierarchy. It is almost as though we frame the servant as being in a position to give something to the person who is being served while that person simply waits passively, having nothing that they, in turn, can give to us. But this notion could not be farther from the truth.

I think that we'd all do well to remind ourselves of our roles as threads in the very same garment, serving to keep *one another* in proper alignment.

In spaces where volunteerism happens among people who are poor, there can be a weird notion that although you are coming to an event or project to serve and offer help or assistance, the people who are helping others who are poor are somehow celebrated as heroes. This type of centering focuses on the volunteers and dismisses those who deserve to be reminded that they too have something to offer the world regardless of their economic status. When I view serving, I view it as a posture of heart to do as Jesus did. He served people without centering on himself. The same message goes on being served in power. Leaders should not belittle or consider those who are doing the service as less than or of little worth. In fact, Paul the apostle writes this switch in perspective of Jesus:

> Let each of you look not only to his own interests, but also to the interests of others. Have this mind among yourselves, which is yours in Christ Jesus, who, though he was in the form of God, did not count equality with God a thing to be grasped, but emptied himself, by taking the form of a servant, being born in the likeness of men. And being found in human form, he humbled himself by becoming obedient to the point of death, even death on a cross. Therefore God has highly exalted him and bestowed on him the

name that is above every name, so that at the name of Jesus every knee should bow, in heaven and on earth and under the earth, and every tongue confess that Jesus Christ is Lord, to the glory of God the Father. (Philippians 2:4-11 ESV)

Those of us who consider ourselves to be possessed by the Holy Spirit believe that we are the ones God has sent into the world to undertake his work. The Bible, of course, tells us that the kingdom of God will one day come to pass, with every tongue and tribe in attendance. If this is all to be taken as truth, then we must live it out in deed— working to help bring about justice for *all*.

To live in the joy of the One who sent us here is to participate in the work that he is already doing: fighting injustice with vigilance, coupled with a refusal to sweep God's heart for justice under the rug. May we not be people who deny the presence of or are shocked by the atrocities leveled against our fellow human beings. Instead, let us seek justice together for our nation and world by being the first to help. In the words popularized by poet June Jordan, "We are the ones we have been waiting for."[3]

ACKNOWLEDGMENTS

S*ankofa* is an African word and the symbol of the Akan tribe in Ghana. The literal translation of the word— and the symbol itself—is a powerful image of a bird with its head turned backward and its body facing forward.

The meanings of both the word and the symbol are powerful. *Sankofa* means to "go back and get it"—or, as the Carter G. Woodson Center at Berea College phrases it, *"it is not taboo to fetch what is at risk of being left behind."*[1] But it can be broken down into three words that have equally important meanings. *San* means "return," *ko* means "go," and *fa* means "to look, seek and take." The power of its meaning lies in part in the idea that we should never, at any moment, forget from where we have come—or what has shaped us.

It is with great honor that I acknowledge the people in my life who have helped me to evolve and become the person I am today. They, collectively, are the reason that I have been able to pen the words in this book.

First, I would like to give special thanks to those people who have supported me along the way, encouraged me, and even sacrificed their time so that I could remember every single moment that God has used to shape my voice, passion, and wisdom.

I would like to acknowledge my wife, Cecilia Lester. Honestly, without your encouragement and inspiration, I wouldn't have been able to push through the many obstacles that I have encountered to be able to undertake the work that our family does each day. You have been my rock and my greatest supporter since I started this journey. I would also like to thank and acknowledge my children, Zion Joy and Terence II, with similar gratitude and thankfulness. Thank you for being amazing children and for always telling me about your dreams of service that you have forged because of the work that our family has committed itself to. You inspire me not only to push harder but also to break every glass ceiling so that you too can have your own *sankofa* moments.

I also would like to give special thanks to my mother, Dr. Connie Walker, for encouraging me to keep chasing my dreams; my sister, Ashley Lester, and her son, Carmelo; and my father, Tyrone Lester, who has become one of my closest friends. I am grateful that God has allowed us to enjoy our talks and our bond in special ways. Many thanks too to my stepfather, Dewitt Walker Sr., for always encouraging me with wisdom and modeling what a life of service looks like. I'd like to acknowledge my grandparents, Carlton and

Gloria York, and Herman and Jessica Lester, for sowing the seeds of resilience and wisdom in my life.

Thanks also goes to the Moore family and the Shaw family, who extended support and encouragement when I was trying to find my way as a teenager.

Special thanks to our friend Brandy Wallner, who helped me to process the ideas found in these pages. My wife and I thank you for your labor of love and support on this journey.

I'd also like to thank my book agent, Tawny Johnson. Thank you for seeing the possibility for and potential of a second book—and for believing that it would be beneficial to those whom it reaches. Thank you, also, for reminding me that I am just getting started.

Special thanks to my editor, Al Hsu. Thank you for being a wonderful guide and believing that I had more to say. Thank you for encouraging me to continue to organize and mobilize people through my words.

A special thank you to the whole IVP family. You truly have given me the space to share my story, from my perspective. For that, I feel at home. Thank you for welcoming me with open arms and for believing that my voice and story matter.

I'd like to thank one of my closest friends, Harvey Strickland, for walking with me, investing in my dreams, and believing that we could change the world through serving—like Jesus. To my friend and brother Mike Fye, thank you for always showing up whenever we were working on projects.

Thanks to the Love Beyond Walls team—every volunteer who has ever served and all those who have supported our advocacy work over the years. Also, a big thanks to my good friend Johnny Taylor for encouraging me and taking part in many of our campaigns to affirm the dignity of those living on the margins.

Thank you to my friend Father Gregory Boyle for encouraging me, sharing wisdom with me, and writing the foreword to this book. Thank you for seeing the value of my words and work.

Thank you all for supporting me and for allowing me to look back on this journey and see how it has pushed the work of God forward.

QUESTIONS FOR REFLECTION AND DISCUSSION

INTRODUCTION: BE BETTER—TOGETHER

1. What does the term "social media trauma" mean to you? Have you ever experienced it? If so, when?

2. If you have experienced social media trauma, did you talk to anyone about the news with which you were confronted, or did you keep it to yourself? If you kept it to yourself, why? And how did your decision to share or not share affect you?

3. In relation to questions one and two, if you have experienced social media trauma, how did the news with which you were confronted make you feel?

4. When you hear about instances of injustice from around the world, does your immediate response tend to lean more toward apathy or taking action?

5. In your opinion, what stands in the way of real, positive change in the world?

6. What does the apostle Paul mean in 1 Corinthians 12:12-27 when he speaks of one body part saying to another, "I have no need of you"?

CHAPTER 1: GET OUT OF YOUR BUBBLE

1. What does it mean to you to become "proximate" to others?

In Romans 12:16 (ESV), Paul exhorts the church to live in community peacefully. The verse says, "Live in harmony with one another. Do not be haughty, but associate with the lowly. Never be wise in your own sight." How has this verse played out in your own interactions with those who might be financially or culturally different from you?

2. In what ways would you say that our lives are interconnected, regardless of questions of race, ethnicity, or socioeconomic status?

3. How does distance affect our perspectives on those who look different from us?

4. How do we interpret these perspectives in light of how Jesus calls us to love people in Mark 12:30-31?

5. Do you believe that you're needed within your community? If not, what would it take to make you believe that you are?

CHAPTER 2: MAKE MORE TIME

1. Would you characterize your life as being overly busy? Name some of the factors that keep your life busy.

2. Why do you think that, in our culture, we tend to glorify having a busy schedule?

3. What would be the top three things on your own "Let Go List"?

4. What keeps you from letting those things go?

5. What is the number one thing that you'd like to start doing?

6. Choose one thing that you'd like to let go of and set a date to do so. If you're participating in these discussion questions in the context of a group, I challenge you to share your specific date for letting go with everyone who is in the group.

CHAPTER 3: PURSUE SOMETHING REAL

1. How would you define the American dream?

2. Is the quest for financial security holding you back from chasing a larger, more meaningful dream? If so, might a change of employment be possible? Could you perhaps downsize your home or reduce the amount that you pay each month by way of bills in order to finance the pursuit of your dream instead?

3. Does your desire for the finer things in life hold you back from embracing your ability to serve others in the way that you could? How has your lifestyle gotten in the way of pursuing the work of God?

4. What aspects of the American dream are at odds with a biblical worldview?

5. What does the term "spiritual poverty" mean to you?

6. Begin to take note of your reactions to social justice issues as you hear about them through the media and in conversation. What is currently stirring up your feelings?

CHAPTER 4: BE BRAVE AND UNLEARN

1. Do you have any unhealthy habits that are holding you back from pursuing your purpose or your meaningful dreams? Name some of these unhealthy habits.

2. How do you practice self-reflection or approach internal work?

3. Have you ever completely changed your opinion about a societal issue after learning new information? If so, explain.

4. Have you ever avoided interaction with someone because of the color of their skin or their economic status? What caused it? Share what happened.

5. Name some of the positive things that could happen to you if you really decided to change the direction of your life, whether personally or professionally.

6. Is there an area of service in which you know that God already wants to use you but that you have been resisting? What has been causing you to resist his will?

CHAPTER 5: THINK "WE"—NOT "ME"

1. How do you define *service*? How do you serve now within your community?

2. In what areas of your life have you failed to notice those whom you could be helping? What would it look like for you to stop and enter into a relationship with them?

3. How do you respond to worldviews that are different from yours?

4. How do you think your response to differing world-views affects your ability to connect and share the love of God with others?

5. How can you leverage your skills or gifts in order to make a meaningful difference in your community?

6. What are the particular issues that your community is currently facing?

CHAPTER 6: KNOW YOUR WORTH
AND MAKE A DIFFERENCE

1. What big change(s) have you wanted to make—either in your career or in terms of your service—but ultimately have not made for fear of judgment or criticism?

2. What would it look like for you to live a life that didn't look like the lives of everyone else whom you know?

3. What kinds of barriers have you encountered in your past attempts to engage in meaningful social justice work or community service?

4. As you start to become aware of the issues in your own community, what ideas about possible solutions or relief are beginning to take shape in your mind?

5. How might you use your abilities to support or participate in a particular movement?

CHAPTER 7: TAKE THE FIRST STEP

1. How have your life experiences shaped you or instilled a passion in you that you could use to serve someone else?

2. If you decided to serve others by using what you have learned through your own experiences, how do you think that your own life might be affected?

3. Who comes to mind when you begin to think about potential allies in your fight for justice? With whom do you need to begin casting a vision?

4. Is there a social injustice story that has lingered with you long after you first heard about it? What was the story?

5. Which issues would you like to learn more about?

6. What does your particular personality type reveal about your possible opportunities to serve?

CHAPTER 8: LIVE INTENTIONALLY

1. How intentional are you when it comes to choosing what to put on your calendar each month?

2. What do you think that Jesus means when he says in John 10:10 that he has come into the world so that we may have life—and have it abundantly? What is "abundant life"?

3. How can you create room for this "abundance" in your own schedule?

4. What proactive planning strategies could you adopt to help you create margins for abundance?

5. Are there activities in your life that keep you "busy"—but are not necessarily meaningful? What are they?

6. What social justice issue have you encountered lately that could be combated if a team were formed in order to do so?

CHAPTER 9: BRING SOMEONE WITH YOU!

1. How does the perception of deficiency affect people's willingness to serve and your willingness to ask others to serve alongside you?

2. What are some of the ways in which Jesus allowed ordinary people to contribute to the extraordinary works of healing and restoration that are described in the Bible?

3. Who are the "orphans" and the "widows" of the modern world?

4. Who are the people in your life who don't recognize just how powerfully they could affect their communities for the better? What gifts and talents do you see in them?

5. How might you encourage the people whom you named in the previous question to join you or to pursue their own lifestyles of service?

6. What steps can you take to become proximate—not just to the people who look like you but to the people whom you see regularly but with whom you don't speak? How can you become proximate to people whom you might have to go out of your way to encounter?

CHAPTER 10: MAXIMIZE YOUR IMPACT

1. How do those who are experiencing financial poverty also experience social poverty?

2. How can creating connections help us maximize our impact?

3. What was the first thing that God deemed to be "not good" in the Bible?

4. In what ways could churches provide better, more extensive social infrastructure to those who are in need?

5. How would you define *compassion?*

6. Would you describe your friends as being similar to you with regard to all demographics (i.e., race, religion, political affiliation)? In what ways?

CONCLUSION: PLAY YOUR PART

1. In times of crisis, how might you start to consider its effects on those who live on the margins of society?

2. When you consider yourself as being a thread in the fabric of a larger garment, connected to others' threads, how does it affect the way in which you see others within the community?

3. What have you learned about yourself in terms of the gifts or skills that you possess and that you could offer to your community?

4. How do you plan on forming new relationships with those who are outside of your typical circle of friends?

5. What steps will you take to become a part of "us" and to serve within—and with—your community?

NOTES

INTRODUCTION: BE BETTER—TOGETHER

[1]Elena Ferrarin, "A Homeless Elgin Man Built Himself an Intricate Abode in the Woods. Now He's Being Evicted from It," Daily Herald, January 3, 2020, www.dailyherald.com/news/20200103/a-homeless-elgin-man-built-himself -an-intricate-abode-in-the-woods-now-hes-being-evicted-from-it.

[2]Vinay Koshy, "61 Social Media Facts and Statistics You Should Know in 2019," Sproutworth, September 19, 2019, www.sproutworth.com/social -media-facts/.

[3]Matt Ford and Adam Chandler, "'Hate Crime': A Mass Killing at a Historic Black Church," Atlantic, June 19, 2015, www.theatlantic.com/national /archive/2015/06/shooting-emanuel-ame-charleston/396209/.

[4]Howard Zinn, A People's History of the United States: 1492-Present (London: Routledge, 2015), 610.

[5]Lewis V. Baldwin and Vicki L. Crawford, Reclaiming the Great World House: The Global Vision of Martin Luther King Jr. (Athens: University of Georgia Press, 2019), 67.

[6]Greg Boyle, Barking to the Choir: The Power of Radical Kinship (New York: Simon & Schuster, 2017), 11.

1. GET OUT OF YOUR BUBBLE

[1]Greg Boyle, Tattoos on the Heart: The Power of Boundless Compassion (New York: Free Press, 2011), 190.

[2]"Martin Luther King Jr.'s 'The Other America' Still Radical 50 Years Later," Beacon Broadside, March 10, 2018, www.beaconbroadside.com /broadside/2018/03/martin-luther-king-jrs-the-other-america-still-radical -50-years-later.html.

[3]If you are unfamiliar with the term gentrification, the most basic definition by Urban Displacement Project is "a process of neighborhood change that includes economic change in a historically disinvested neighborhood—by

means of real estate investment and new higher-income residents moving in—as well as demographic change—not only in terms of income level, but also in terms of changes in the education level or racial make-up of residents" ("Gentrification Explained," Urban Displacement Project, accessed August 22, 2020, www.urbandisplacement.org/gentrification-explained).

⁴Elena Renken, "Most Americans Are Lonely, and Our Workplace Culture May Not Be Helping," NPR, January 23, 2020, www.npr.org/sections/health -shots/2020/01/23/798676465/most-americans-are-lonely-and-our-work place-culture-may-not-be-helping.

⁵Jennifer Latson, "A Cure for Disconnection," *Psychology Today,* March 7, 2018, www.psychologytoday.com/us/articles/201803/cure-disconnection.

⁶Martin Luther King Jr., "Letter from a Birmingham Jail," The Martin Luther King, Jr. Research and Education Institute, accessed January 30, 2020, https://kinginstitute.stanford.edu/king-papers/documents/letter -birmingham-jail.

⁷"Martin Luther King, Jr.'s 'A Christmas Sermon on Peace' Still Prophetic 50 Years Later," Beacon Broadside, December 24, 2017, www.beaconbroadside .com/broadside/2017/12/martin-luther-king-jrs-christmas-sermon-peace -still-prophetic-50-years-later.html.

⁸Michelle Martin, "No 'Us and Them' Is Cure to Violence, Speaker Says," *Chicago Catholic,* April 24, 2019, www.chicagocatholic.com/chicagoland /-/article/2019/04/24/no-us-and-them-is-cure-to-violence-speaker-says.

⁹According to definition sites, the traditional definition of *proximity* means "closeness" or "next to"; however, we take that word to only mean in terms of distance and space. When I speak of the word *proximity*, I am talking about getting close to others in a relational way. Proximity helps us move past the superficial view of people and helps us to know people more deeply. In fact, you can't know who you are not proximate to. Proximity is the ultimate statement of what it means to be a neighbor to someone. It is the call of God to love our neighbor as ourselves. We cannot do that apart from proximity. Proximity is the invitation to live fully engaged in community with those where God has placed or called you to. There is no real change apart from it.

¹⁰Roman Krznaric, "Six Habits of Highly Empathetic People," *Greater Good Magazine,* November 27, 2012, https://greatergood.berkeley.edu/article /item/six_habits_of_highly_empathic_people1.

¹¹Larry Osborne, *Accidental Pharisees: Avoiding Pride, Exclusivity, and The Other Dangers of Overzealous Faith* (Grand Rapids, MI: Zondervan, 2012), 75.

2. MAKE MORE TIME

[1]Caroline Beaton, "When Your Schedule Is Sick: Three Busyness Disorders That Make Us Anxious and Unsatisfied," *Forbes*, June 3, 2016, www.forbes .com/sites/carolinebeaton/2016/05/25/when-your-schedule-is-sick-three -busyness-disorders-that-make-us-anxious-and-unsatisfied.

[2]Sarah Pulliam Bailey, "'I Feel So Distant from God': Popular D.C.-Area Pastor Confesses He's Tired, Announces Sabbatical," *Washington Post*, December 11, 2019, www.washingtonpost.com/religion/2019/12/11/i-feel-so-distant-god -popular-dc-area-pastor-confesses-hes-tired-announces-sabbatical/.

[3]Emily P. Freeman, *The Next Right Thing: A Simple, Soulful Practice for Making Life Decisions* (Grand Rapids, MI: Revell, 2019).

[4]Michelle Braden, "Busyness Is Our Worst Addiction," *Forbes*, December 6, 2018, www.forbes.com/sites/forbescoachescouncil/2018/12/06/busyness -is-our-worst-addiction/#7c1b1d872215.

[5]Braden, "Busyness Is Our Worst Addiction."

3. PURSUE SOMETHING REAL

[1]"What Is Modern Slavery?," Anti-Slavery International, accessed January 31, 2020, www.antislavery.org/slavery-today/modern-slavery/.

[2]Council of Economic Advisors, *The State of Homelessness in America* (Washington, DC: Executive Office of the United States, 2019), www.whitehouse.gov /wp-content/uploads/2019/09/The-State-of-Homelessness-in-America.pdf.

[3]Jason Silverstein, "There Were More Mass Shootings Than Days in 2019," CBS News, January 2, 2020, www.cbsnews.com/news/mass-shootings -2019-more-than-days-365/.

[4]Sarah Anderson, ed., *The Souls of Poor Folk: A Preliminary Report* (Washington, DC: Institute of Policy Studies, 2017), www.poorpeoplescampaign.org /wp-content/uploads/2017/12/PPC-Report-Draft-1.pdf.

[5]*Minimalism: A Documentary About the Important Things*, directed by Matt D'Avella (Catalyst, 2016).

[6]Jenny Santi, "The Secret to Happiness Is Helping Others," *TIME*, August 4, 2017, https://time.com/4070299/secret-to-happiness/.

[7]Joshua Becker, "You Don't Need More Things in Your Life. You Need Different Things," *Becoming Minimalist* (blog), accessed January 21, 2020, www .becomingminimalist.com/subtract/.

4. BE BRAVE AND UNLEARN

[1]Tonya Russell, "How Black and White Families Are Talking about Racism in a Time of Reckoning," June 3, 2020, *Washington Post*, www.washingtonpost.com /lifestyle/2020/06/03/how-do-families-talk-about-racism-with-their-kids/.
[2]Henri Nouwen, *The Wounded Healer: Ministry in Contemporary Society* (New York: Crown Publishing Group, 2013), 72.
[3]Jennifer Ouellette, "What Does It Take to Change a Mind? A Phase Transition," *Cocktail Party Physics* (blog), *Scientific American*, February 13, 2015, https://blogs.scientificamerican.com/cocktail-party-physics/what-does-it -take-to-change-a-mind-a-phase-transition/.

5. THINK "WE"—NOT "ME"

[1]Martin Luther King Jr., "The Other America," speech, Memorial Auditorium, Stanford University, April 14, 1967, Stanford, CA, The Martin Luther King, Jr. Research and Education Institute, https://kinginstitute.stanford.edu /news/50-years-ago-martin-luther-king-jr-speaks-stanford-university.
[2]*Encyclopaedia Britannica Online*, s.v. "Pharisee," accessed May 22, 2020, www .britannica.com/topic/Pharisee.
[3]Erik Raymond, "Pastors, Platforms, and Pride," *Ordinary Pastor* (blog), The Gospel Coalition, May 4, 2016, www.thegospelcoalition.org/blogs/erik-raymond/pastors-platforms-and-pride/.
[4]Martin Luther King Jr., "The Drum Major Instinct," sermon, Ebenezer Baptist Church, February 4, 1968, Atlanta, GA, The Martin Luther King, Jr. Research and Education Institute, https://kinginstitute.stanford.edu/king -papers/documents/drum-major-instinct-sermon-delivered-ebenezer -baptist-church.
[5]King Jr., "The Drum Major Instinct."
[6]Jasmine Crowe, "Hunger Is Not a Question of Scarcity," TEDxPeachtree, October 2017, video, 14:51, www.ted.com/talks/jasmine_crowe_hunger_is _not_a_question_of_scarcity.
[7]Crowe, "Hunger Is Not a Question."
[8]Adedamola Agboola, "Atlanta-Based Innovation and Leadership Center Names James Bailey New CEO," Black Enterprise, March 28, 2018, www .blackenterprise.com/james-jay-bailey-appointed-ceo-of-the-russell-center/.
[9]"Love and Purpose—Don & Cierra 'Fly' Bobo," interview by Rhonda Glaze, August 8, 2018, video, 56:33, www.youtube.com/watch?v=j3glDzUxspM&t=320s.

[10]"Curriculum," FLY Life, accessed February 6, 2020, http://theflylife.org/curriculum/.

[11]Jelani Cobb, "William Barber Takes on Poverty and Race in the Age of Trump," New Yorker, May 7, 2018, www.newyorker.com/magazine/2018/05/14/william-barber-takes-on-poverty-and-race-in-the-age-of-trump.

[12]"Our Principles," Poor People's Campaign: A National Call for Moral Revival, accessed February 7, 2020, www.poorpeoplescampaign.org/about/our-principles/.

6. KNOW YOUR WORTH AND MAKE A DIFFERENCE

[1]History.com editors, "Montgomery Bus Boycott," HISTORY, updated February 10, 2020, www.history.com/topics/black-history/montgomery-bus-boycott.

[2]History.com editors, "Montgomery Bus Boycott."

[3]"In Real Life: Join the Movement," MENTOR: The National Mentoring Partnership, accessed February 18, 2020, www.mentoring.org/in-real-life/.

[4]Find out more at www.happynpo.com/about/.

[5]The Happy Givers (Shopify), available online at https://thehappygivers.com, accessed February 12, 2020.

[6]Find out more at www.happynpo.com/relief.

[7]Find out more at https://realjusticepac.org.

[8]Hunter Moyler, "Free Rodney Reed Petition Nears 3 Million Signatures As Scheduled Execution of Death Row Inmate Approaches," Newsweek, November 14, 2019, www.newsweek.com/free-rodney-reed-petition-nears-3-million-signatures-scheduled-execution-death-row-inmate-1471791.

[9]"Shaun King: We Need Your Help to Save Rodney Reed," November 7, 2019, video, 9:16, www.youtube.com/watch?v=ReSO_ZEBz48&feature=emb_title.

[10]Mike Maciag, "The Citizens Most Vocal in Local Government," Governing, July 2014, www.governing.com/topics/politics/gov-national-survey-shows-citizens-most-vocal-active-in-local-government.html.

[11]Angela Hanks, Danyelle Solomon, and Christian E. Weller, "Systematic Inequality: How America's Structural Racism Helped Create the Black-White Wealth Gap," Center for American Progress, February 21, 2018, www.american-progress.org/issues/race/reports/2018/02/21/447051/systematic-inequality/.

7. TAKE THE FIRST STEP

[1]Abdul Razaq et al., "BAME COVID-19 DEATHS—What Do We Know? Rapid Data & Evidence Review," Oxford University Centre for Evidence-Based

Medicine (CEBM), May 5, 2020, www.cebm.net/covid-19/bame-covid-19-deaths-what-do-we-know-rapid-data-evidence-review/.

[2]Marian Knight, ed., et al., "Saving Lives, Improving Mothers' Care: Lessons Learned to Inform Maternity Care from the UK and Ireland Confidential Enquiries into Maternal Deaths and Morbidity 2015-17," Nuffield Department of Population Health (NPEU), November 2019, www.npeu.ox.ac.uk /assets/downloads/mbrrace-uk/reports/MBRRACE-UK%20Maternal %20Report%202019%20-%20WEB%20VERSION.pdf.

[3]Mary Beth Flanders-Stepans, "Alarming Racial Differences in Maternal Mortality," *Journal of Perinatal Education* 9, no. 2 (Spring 2000): 50-51, www.ncbi .nlm.nih.gov/pmc/articles/PMC1595019/.

[4]Colleen Walsh, "'Me Too Founder Discusses Where We Go from Here': Advocate and Activist Tarana Burke to Receive the Harvard Kennedy School's Center for Public Leadership Gleitsman Award," *Harvard Gazette*, February 21, 2020, https://news.harvard.edu/gazette/story/2020/02/me-too -founder-tarana-burke-discusses-where-we-go-from-here/.

[5]Monica Anderson and Skye Toor, "How Social Media Users Have Discussed Sexual Harassment Since #MeToo Went Viral," Pew Research Center, October 11, 2018, www.pewresearch.org/fact-tank/2018/10/11/how-social-media -users-have-discussed-sexual-harassment-since-metoo-went-viral/.

[6]Lauren M. Johnson, "A Los Angeles Church Is Paying Off $5.3 Million of Medical Debt in Its Community," CNN, December 24, 2019, www.cnn .com/2019/12/24/us/church-medical-debt-payoff-trnd/index.html.

[7]"Medical Debt Pay-Off," Christian Assembly, accessed February 20, 2020, https://cachurch.com/weekend-services/medicaldebtpayoff/.

[8]Sarah Corbett, "Activism Needs Introverts," TEDxYouth@Bath, November 2016, video, 13:49, www.ted.com/talks/sarah_corbett_activism_needs_introverts.

[9]Isaac Chotiner, "A Black Lives Matter Co-Founder Explains Why This Time Is Different," *New Yorker*, June 3, 2020, www.newyorker.com/news/q-and-a /a-black-lives-matter-co-founder-explains-why-this-time-is-different.

[10]Emma Watson, "Gender Equality Is Your Issue Too" (speech, special event for the HeForShe campaign, UN Headquarters, New York, NY, September 20, 2014), www.unwomen.org/en/news/stories/2014/9/emma-watson-gender -equality-is-your-issue-too.

[11]UN Women, *2019 Impact Report: HeForShe*, accessed February 20, 2020, www.heforshe.org/sites/default/files/2019-12/HFS_IMPACT_2019_ Onscreen_revised.pdf.

[12]"A Level Playing Field for Kids," HeForShe, accessed February 20, 2020, www .heforshe.org/en/level-playing-field-kids.

[13]See www.volunteermatch.org for more information.

[14]Find out more at purposity.com.

8. LIVE INTENTIONALLY

[1]John Lewis, "Do not get lost in a sea of despair. Do not become bitter or hostile. Be hopeful, be optimistic. Never, ever be afraid to make some noise and get in good trouble, necessary trouble. We will find a way to make a way out of no way. #goodtrouble," Twitter, July 16, 2019, https://twitter.com /repjohnlewis/status/1151155571757867011?lang=en.

[2]Jiawen Chen et al., "Wanting to Be Remembered: Intrinsically Rewarding Work and Generativity in Early Midlife," *Canadian Review of Sociology* 56, no. 1 (February 2019), 30-48, https://doi.org/https://doi.org/10.1111/cars.12228.

[3]See http://jimmystarnes.com.

[4]Maya Chung, "Formerly Homeless Woman Now Giving Back to Other Women in Her Community," Inside Edition, August 11, 2017, www.inside edition.com/headlines/24908-formerly-homeless-woman-now-giving-back -to-other-women-in-her-community.

[5]Giving Hands Salon, givinghandsbeautysalon.com, more online at https://parade.com/636168/lharris-2/youll-never-guess-why-this-beauty -salon-owner-is-giving-makeovers-to-needy-women/, accessed March 3, 2020.

[6]John-Mark Comer, *The Ruthless Elimination of Hurry*, read by John-Mark Comer and Kris Koscheski (New York: Random House Audio, 2019), Audible audio ed., 5 hr., 20 min.

9. BRING SOMEONE WITH YOU!

[1]K. A. Ellis, "Loving the Widow in the 21st Century," *The Gospel Coalition Podcast*, August 3, 2018, www.thegospelcoalition.org/podcasts/tgc-podcast /loving-widow-21st-century/.

[2]Jason Fried and David Heinemeier Hansson, *Rework* (New York: Crown Publishing Group, 2019).

[3]Katie Shepherd, "Louisville Bans 'No-Knock' Warrants After Police Killing of Breonna Taylor Inside Her Home," *Washington Post*, June 12, 2020, www .washingtonpost.com/nation/2020/06/12/louisville-breonna-taylor-law/.

[4]"CNN Honors 10 Men and Women for Making the World a Better Place,"
CNN, December 7, 2019, www.cnn.com/2019/10/30/world/cnn-heroes-top
-ten-2019/index.html.

[5]Find out more at www.vamosladies.com.

10. MAXIMIZE YOUR IMPACT

[1]Brené Brown, *Daring Greatly: How the Courage to Be Vulnerable Transforms the
Way We Live, Love, Parent, and Lead* (New York: Avery, 2012), 10.

[2]Brown, *Daring Greatly*.

[3]Saoirse Kerrigan, "15 Examples of 'Anti-Homeless' Hostile Architecture That
You Probably Never Noticed Before," Interesting Engineering, May 22, 2018,
https://interestingengineering.com/15-examples-anti-homeless-hostile-
architecture-that-you-probably-never-noticed-before.

[4]Eric Klinenberg, "Palaces for the People: How Social Infrastructure Can Help
Fight Inequality, Polarization, and the Decline of Civic Life," Talks at Google,
January 17, 2019, video, 59:25, www.youtube.com/watch?v=HJIYhSA84Sc.

[5]"Hypothermia Deaths Spike After the Closing of Atlanta Homeless Shelter,"
Valdosta Today, December 2, 2019, https://valdostatoday.com/news-2
/region/2019/12/hypothermia-deaths-spike-after-the-closing-of-atlanta
-homeless-shelter/.

[6]"San Franciscans Raise $70,000 to Stop Homeless Shelter in Wealthy Area,"
The Guardian, March 29, 2019, www.theguardian.com/us-news/2019/mar
/28/san-francisco-gofundme-homeless-shelter-embarcadero.

[7]"Dying Alone: An Interview with Eric Klinenberg" (Chicago: University of
Chicago Press, 2002), www.press.uchicago.edu/Misc/Chicago/443213in.html,
accessed March 13, 2020..

[8]"Dying Alone."

[9]Laura Scholz, "My Style: So Worth Loving Founder Eryn Erickson," *Atlanta*,
April 26, 2016, www.atlantamagazine.com/style/style-eryn-erickson/.

[10]Eryn Erickson, personal correspondence with author, March 12, 2020.

[11]Henri J. M. Nouwen, Donald P. McNeill, and Douglas A. Morrison, *Compassion:
A Reflection on the Christian Life* (Garden City, NY: Doubleday, 2006), 4.

[12]"U.S. Adults Have Few Friends—and They're Mostly Alike," Barna, October
23, 2018, www.barna.com/research/friends-loneliness/.

[13]"U.S. Adults Have Few Friends."

[14]Emily Esfahani Smith, "Social Connection Makes a Better Brain," *Atlantic*,

October 29, 2013, www.theatlantic.com/health/archive/2013/10/social
-connection-makes-a-better-brain/280934.

CONCLUSION: PLAY YOUR PART

[1]Terence Lester, *I See You: How Love Opens Our Eyes to Invisible People* (Downers
Grove, IL: InterVarsity Press, 2019), 14-15.

[2]Find out more about Father Boyle's ministry, Homeboy Industries, at home
boyindustries.org.

[3]June Jordan, "Poem for South African Women," quoted in Alice Walker, *We
Are the Ones We Have Been Waiting For* (New York: New Press, 2006), 3.

ACKNOWLEDGMENTS

[1]"The Power of Sankofa: Know History," Berea College, accessed August 21,
2020, www.berea.edu/cgwc/the-power-of-sankofa.

Terence Lester is the founder and executive director of Love Beyond Walls, and the author of *I See You: How Love Opens Our Eyes to Invisible People*. He is a community activist, minister, speaker, and author. He believes that all people deserve equity, love, and a chance to change their lives. Terence travels domestically and internationally speaking about issues relating to social justice, poverty, homelessness, faith, and culture. His awareness campaigns on behalf of the poor have been featured in *USA Today*, *Atlanta Journal-Constitution*, *Black Enterprise*, *Rolling Out*, on NBC and Upworthy, and have been viewed by over ten million people globally. His greatest passion involves educating the general public about pressing issues that plague the lives of those who are vulnerable and voiceless and using the educational piece to mobilize an army of people to love and serve those who are unseen. Terence holds four degrees and has written several books. He is happily married to Cecilia, and together they have two wonderful children, Zion Joy and Terence II.

terencelester.com
twitter.com/imterencelester
facebook.com/imterencelester
instagram.com/imterencelester

ABOUT LOVE
BEYOND WALLS

Love Beyond Walls is a movement birthed out of the hope that love is greater than walls. One of the most distinguishable characteristics of our organization is our focus on telling the stories of the unseen. We are committed to people that the world passes by because we believe the people struggling with poverty and sleeping on the streets have lives and stories that are just as valuable as ours.

We exist to provide dignity to the homeless and poor by providing a voice, visibility, shelter, community, grooming, and support services to achieve self-sufficiency.

Address: 3270 East Main Street, College Park, GA 30337
Email: info@lovebeyondwalls.org
lovebeyondwalls.org
twitter.com/lovebeyondwalls
facebook.com/lovebeyondwalls
vimeo.com/lovebeyondwalls
instagram.com/lovebeyondwalls